THE ART
QUILT COLLECTION

Introduction © 2010 by Linda Seward

Produced for Sixth&Spring Books by Penn Publishing Ltd.

www.penn.co.il

Editor-in-Chief: Rachel Penn

Editor: Shoshana Brickman

Design and layout: Ariane Rybski

ISBN-10: 1-936096-08-0

ISBN-13: 978-1-936096-08-4

Library of Congress Control Number: 2010921213

Manufactured in China

THE ART
QUILT COLLECTION

Designs & Inspiration from Around the World

FOREWORD BY
LINDA SEWARD

sixth&spring
books

GALLERY OF ARTIST'S QUILTS

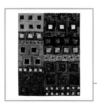

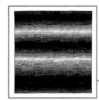

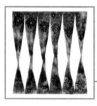
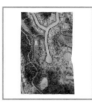

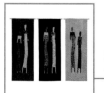

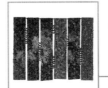

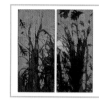

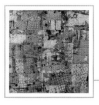

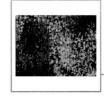

FOREWORD

LINDA SEWARD

Every quilt is a work of art, but there is a difference between a quilt made as a functional bed covering and a quilt made for display on a wall or as a freestanding object. In the past, women made quilts for use in the home. While these were pleasing objects in their own right, they were certainly not considered "art." These quilts were displayed with pride but always on beds and therefore in rooms that were usually not seen by the general public. The "best quilts" were those made only in good light using the finest fabrics and tiniest stitches. These were reserved for special occasions such as a wedding night or visits from the doctor or minister, and because these quilts were used so rarely, many survive to this day in excellent condition. This tells us how much these quilts were valued for their workmanship and the time spent making them, but it doesn't convey whether the pieces were prized for their artistic merit. The quilt makers themselves had to know they had created a masterpiece, but this wasn't acknowledged the way,

for example, a painting would have been. Quilted art simply did not have the same value as other forms of art. As quilt maker Charlotte Yde so aptly says, "Stitches seem subversive in the fine art world."

Well, thankfully all of that is changing. In 1971, the Whitney Museum of American Art in New York held an exhibition of Amish quilts and since then, quilts have been looked at in a different light and valued as works of art rather than mere functional objects. And as quilting enjoyed a resurgence in popularity in the United States and subsequently all over the world, quilt makers began exploring ways of making their work more exciting—taking quilts off beds and hanging them firmly on walls. Traditional cotton fabrics were augmented with the use of silk, linen, wool, hessian, scrim, synthetics, paper and even plastic. Techniques from other needlework and craft disciplines, such as dyeing, printing, stamping, silk screening, stenciling, painting, burning, fabric manipulation and distressing, discharging and wax resists were incorporated into quilts. Quilt makers enjoyed embroidering and embellishing their work, adding yet another dimension. "I revel in accident and experimentation," states Cynthia Corbin, who probably speaks for most of the quilt makers featured in this book.

While traditional quilters use technical skill and a replication of long-established patterns as a focus for their work, art quilters have modified conventional techniques to suit their own requirements. The visual impact of their work is of utmost importance, and while skillful stitching is expected, it isn't the most significant aspect of an art quilt. Conveying a message, celebrating an idea or concept and attempting to touch the spirit and soul of the viewer have much more relevance.

The excitement of looking at art quilts lies in their utter diversity—each one is as different as its maker. Barbara Olson sums it up nicely when she asks, "Which idea should I give life to?" Inspirations come from every walk of life and art quilters are not afraid to tell it like it is. Political statements jostle with landscapes and geometric puzzles; color studies are juxtaposed with realistic portrayals of plants, animals and people. Art quilts are always surprising and never mundane—each is a revelation, and viewers will discover something new every time they look at one.

This book features the work of artists from all over the world, proving beyond a doubt that quilt-making is truly international. The sheer imagination and exuberance of these pieces attest to the joy that these talented makers clearly feel when engaging in their work. Interspersed throughout are excellent step-by-step instructions for replicating various imaginative techniques, enabling quilters to incorporate new methods into their own work—exactly the concept behind creating an art quilt.

You'll want to peruse this book time and again for the pleasure of seeing the delightful quilts, for the enjoyment of the designs and also for inspiration. Relax, sit back and treat yourself to a remarkable collection of work by some of today's finest international quilt artists.

The QUILTS

ENERGIE

White and black cotton satin;
appliquéd and hand quilted;
83 x 83 inches (211 x 211 cm)

ADELHEID GUBSER
Cornol, Switzerland

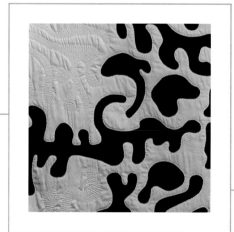

*My preferred material is textile because
it is soft and warm, but can also be
cool. My quilts are mostly worked by
hand to preserve the special properties
of the textile. Another fascinating
element of textiles is their history; the
marvelous processes and touching
stories about how items such as cotton
and silk are produced.*

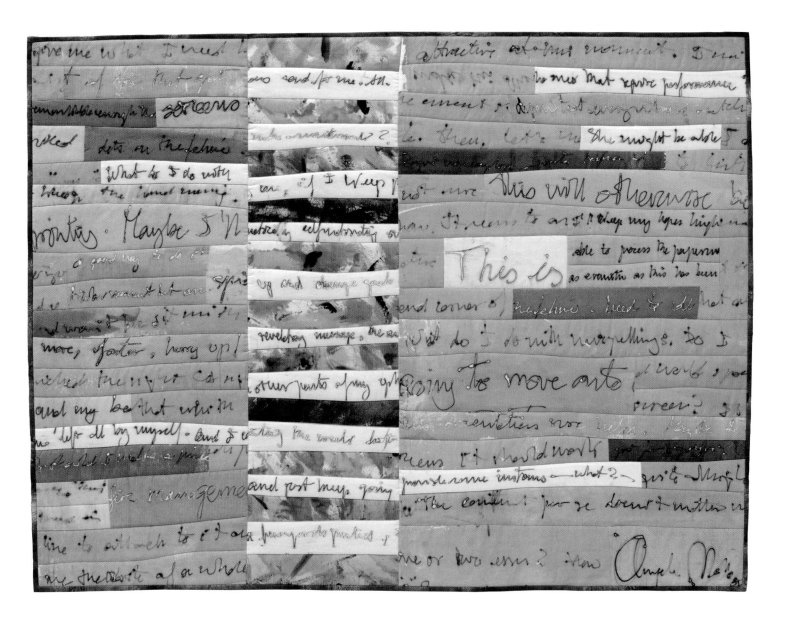

SECRET DIARY 19: "MORE, FASTER, HURRY UP!"

Dyes, cotton; screen printed and painted,
machine pieced and quilted;
48 x 36 inches (122 x 91 cm)

ANGELA MOLL
Santa Barbara, California, USA

I am looking inside, into the intimate space where journals are written, where quilts are stitched. The pages of my Secret Diaries are journal entries, screen printed onto fabric. The text records the flow of thoughts as I write on the screen with fabric dye. The collaged and stitched diary fragments speak about intimacy and communication, as well as privacy and isolation.

THE BLACK BOX

Commercial fabric; raw-edge collaged,
machine quilted, hand embroidered;
16 x 16 x 16 inches (41 x 41 x 41 cm)

BETTINA ANDERSEN
Copenhagen, Denmark

*When an airplane or ship has been in
a catastrophe, authorities search for the
black box to find out what happened. In
this quilt, the black box is a metaphor
for human beings. And no, it's not
entirely black. Often, we are quick
to decide what we think about each
other; a closer look often reveals more
complexity and differences.*

TWILIGHT AND STRIPES

Cotton, striped fabrics; machine
pieced, machine quilted,
appliquéd and embroidered;
51 x 56 inches (130 x 142 cm)

GABRIELLE PAQUIN
Orléans, France

*My art quilts are created for the pleasure
of experimenting with lines, colors and
forms with striped fabrics. I like to search
original designs, playing and contrasting
lines and curves. In the past, striped
fabrics had a negative feeling, and this
aspect remains in quilting. This was
another reason for me (the first one is that
I like stripes) to use them as a challenge.*

CENTRAL PARK WEST BEFORE DAWN

Cotton, textile paints; painted,
printed, machine pieced;
44 x 53 inches (112 x 135 cm)

LINDA LEVIN
Wayland, Massachusetts, USA

The inspiration for my work comes from places I've seen and stored away in my memory. I don't try to capture a specific scene, but an atmosphere, a mood or a moment. This quilt features abstracted views of New York City.

SENEGAL

African shibori cotton, hand-dyed cotton,
commercial batik; reverse appliquéd
with *passepoil*, intensively quilted;
three pieces, 14 + 17 + 15 x 53 inches
(36 cm + 43 cm + 38 cm x 160 cm)

MONIQUE GILBERT-OVERSTEYNS
Bierbeek, Belgium

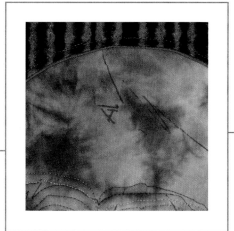

*I bought the fabric for this quilt at a
local market in Senegal. The fabric is
used for traditional men's clothing,
and was sold in two pieces. I used one
piece to make this triptych. The African
symbols are quilted in dark blue.*

CELLULAR STRUCTURE VI

Silk, cotton, polyester, commercial
and found fabrics, recycled clothing;
dyed, painted, fused, monoprinted,
machine quilted;
40 x 81 inches (102 x 206 cm)

SUE BENNER
Dallas, Texas, USA

*Structure and organization exist on
multiple levels, from the subatomic to the
cosmic. In this series, I think about the
layering of structure and looking deeply
to see what is beyond the surface. A cell
can be described as the functional unit
of a larger whole. The biological cell is
particularly fascinating to me. These
shapes live in my mind and are the
building blocks of my world and art.*

NAUTILUS
LONGLIFE

Cotton, silk thread; computer designed,
printed on fabric, machine sewed, free
machine embroidered, machine quilted;
38 x 38 inches (97 x 97 cm)

VERENA MATTER
Schönau, Hütten, Switzerland

*The nautilus is a symbol for long life,
and what else does a mother wish for
her children? I was visiting my daughter
in Hawaii when she turned 20, and
of course I was a bit worried. At home
again, I had some beautiful pictures I
had taken there and I worked with them,
and my thoughts were woven in the
embroidered part.*

TULIPS

Wide range of fabrics, including hand-dyed cottons, polyester organza, polyester, velvet, glittery fabric, chocolate wrappers; appliquéd, free machine quilted;
57 x 39 inches (145 x 99 cm)

INEKE BERLYN
Bromsgrove, United Kingdom

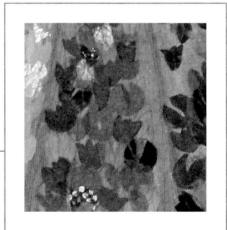

I spend many hours wandering around the Netherlands airport waiting to fly back to the UK and almost always end up buying a postcard of tulip fields. One such postcard inspired this quilt. The tulip petals were cut from all kinds of fabrics. To make life even more difficult, I appliquéd both the back and front of the quilt, for a two-sided effect.

WILD CHILD

Commercial cottons, thread;
machine appliquéd, machine quilted;
40 x 40 inches (102 x 102 cm)

BARBARA OLSON
Billings, Montana, USA

I found myself with some uninterrupted studio time and the question was "which idea should I give life to?" A simple flower drawing was a good place to start. In a playful gesture, I pulled out all my wild novelty prints and began with the fabric I loved most. The design grew from that first choice. The image has a tremendous WOW factor.

DRESS CODE BLACK
(THE SUBVERSIVE STITCHES)

Cotton, tulle, translucent organdy;
quilted, burned, digital and free-motion
machine embroidered;
16 x 16 inches (40 x 40 cm)

CHARLOTTE YDE
Frederiksberg, Denmark

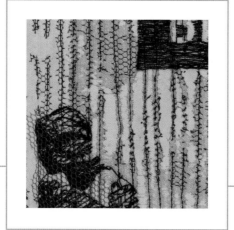

Ever since I was little, I have loved fabric, preferably an abundance of it. This is one of the reasons I have always been drawn to clothing from other cultures. I treasure democracy, individual freedom and freedom of speech, and all of these aspects come together in this work. The title refers to politics, as well as the fact that stitches seem subversive in the fine-art world.

24

OBSESSION

Cotton fabric, batting; hand dyed by the
artist, cut very freely, assembled in quarter
blocks, machine pieced, machine quilted;
72 x 96 inches (183 x 244 cm)

ELLIN LARIMER
Port Ludlow, Washington, USA

*I am interested in exploring the
relationships of lines and shapes while
direct piecing quilts and combining
colors in an exciting manner. I dye
my own cotton; it is a continuous
experiment and surprise. I machine
piece and quilt my own work.*

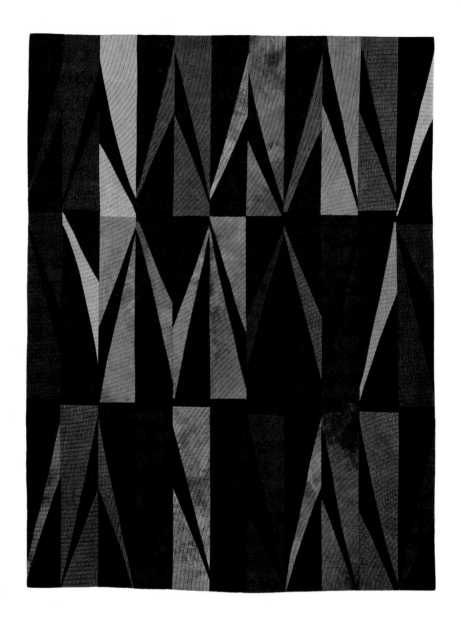

WINGED VICTORY

Hand-dyed cotton; cut freehand,
machine pieced, machine quilted;
47 x 63 inches (120 x 160 cm)

JANET STEADMAN
Langley, Washington, USA

*I find each step of quilt making, from
beginning to end, a real challenge, and
it is hard to say which part I like best.
I love the pure creativity involved in
conceiving and designing a new quilt.
I love to piece, and most of my quilts
are made that way. Most of my work is
machine quilted, although I often add
seed stitching done by hand.*

ASPEN FIRE

Hand-dyed and commercial cotton and
silk fabrics; machine pieced and quilted,
direct appliquéd, silkscreened;
24 x 40 inches (61 x 102 cm)

JUDITH TOMLINSON TRAGER
Boulder, Colorado, USA

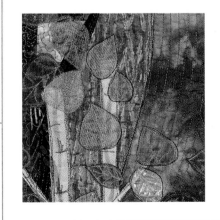

*My work celebrates the complexity
and ambiguity of the contemporary
landscape that I see around me—the
natural landscape overlaid with the built
environment, the changes growth brings
to the landscape and human settlement,
the changes in my work brought by my
physical ability. My landscapes are of
dreams and immediacy, my narratives
are of past lives and future commitments.*

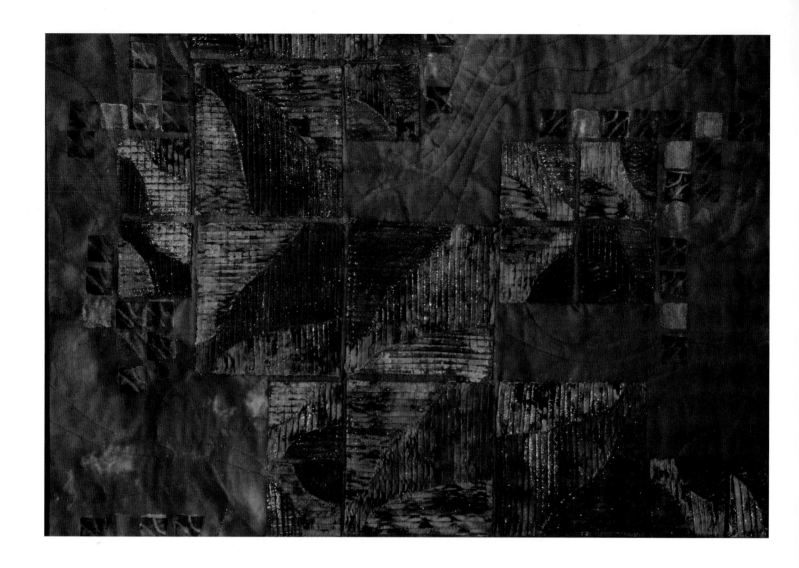

FLOW

Hand-dyed and commercial fabric;
pleated, machine stitched, machine quilted;
33 x 43 inches (84 x 109 cm)

ITA ZIV
Pardes Hana, Israel

*My work is inspired by things from daily
life, personal experiences, the natural
world and political situations. Small
joys and large ones, the beauty of flowers
rejuvenated after a rainfall, nature's
remarkable ability to recover, sunrises
and sunsets, memories, sadness, pain,
fulfillment, anger, hurt, hope, love and the
passion of inspiration, to name a few.*

STEP-BY-STEP: PLEATED BLOCKS

In *Flow* (opposite page), fabric blocks are pleated then machine sewn to secure the pleats. These blocks a[...]
groups of three, and each stack is cut into three pieces. These pieces are rearranged to make tricolor plea[...]

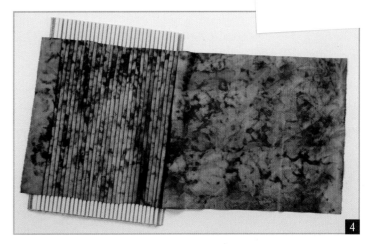

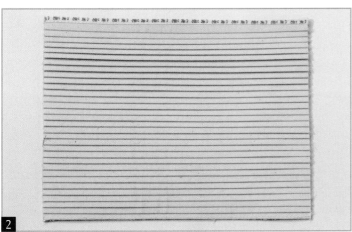

1. Select the fabric for your quilt.

2. Lay the pleater on your work surface with the louver openings facing away from you.

3. Trim the fabric pieces so that they are about ½ inch (1.3 cm) narrower than the pleater. This gives you space to lift the folds and tuck in the fabric.

4. Lay the fabric on the pleater, wrong side up, and tuck it into the louvers. Make sure the fabric reaches the bottom of each louver.

5. When all the fabric has been tucked, or when the pleater is full, lay a piece of fusible stabilizer over the fabric, and press with an iron.

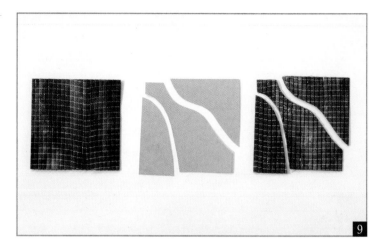

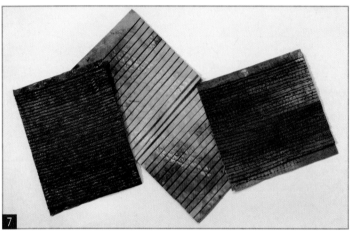

6. When the fabric has cooled completely, remove it from the pleater by peeling it away.

7. Repeat steps 3 to 6 to pleat all of the fabric for the pleated blocks. To make larger pleats, use the same pleater, but tuck the fabric into every other louver.

8. Cut the pleated blocks into squares and machine sew each square with straight lines.

9. Draw the pattern for each block onto a square of Bristol board. Cut the Bristol board and trace the pieces onto three pleated fabric squares that are the same size. Cut the squares.

10. Arrange the cut pieces of fabric into tricolored blocks, orienting the pleats as desired.

11. When all of the blocks are complete, lay the background fabric on you work surface. Arranged the blocks on top, securing them in place with small dots of fabric glue in the corners.

12. When you are satisfied with the composition, sew the pieces in place using transparent thread. ■

RUNDY

Cotton fabric, fusible web, assorted threads;
raw-edge appliquéd, thread painted, quilted;
41 x 50 inches (104 x 127 cm)

MARILYN BELFORD
Chenango Forks, New York, USA

*Aristotle said, "The quality of life is
determined by its activities." Happiness
in this life is something to do, and to
love what you are doing. Teaching and
creating art quilts is my happiness.
Quilting has afforded me the means
and tools with which to express my
visions. Creativity is not dependent on
inherited talent. It is within the very
soul of every human being.*

BETWEEN
EARTH AND SKY

Silk, dyes, embroidery thread;
hand dyed with resists, silkscreen
printed, discharge dyed, hand pieced,
embroidered, hand quilted;
32 x 54 inches (81 x 137 cm)

NANCY WHITTINGTON
Chapel Hill, North Carolina, USA

*This work explores the dual nature of the
worlds we live between: earth and sky. We
belong to the solid ground, which contains
the secret forms of seeds. We belong to the
sky, the place of breath and cosmic forms,
which generate wind, water and light.
The symbolism of this contrasting yet
symbiotic union is expressed in this quilt's
two opposing colors: yellow and blue.*

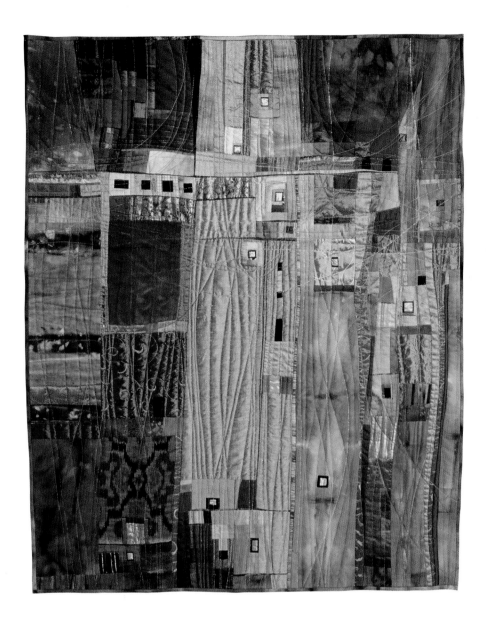

JOURNEYS 4: NIGHT FLIGHT

Commercial and hand-dyed cotton, silk, taffeta, brocade, velvet; machine and hand pieced and appliquéd, machine quilted; 31 x 38 inches (78 x 96 cm)

ROSALIE DACE
Durban, South Africa

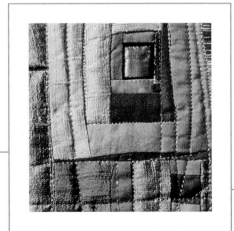

I made this quilt to deal with my anxiety about going on a long trip. I thought longingly about the long flight home, when the plane comes in low over Durban Harbor a few minutes before landing. I would be able to see the lights of ships, buildings and streets shimmering on the water. The excitement of that view is almost unbearable. I am nearly home.

CASTLE WALL

Cotton; machine stitched, hand
appliquéd, hand quilted;
75 x 64 inches (190 x 163 cm)

TRUDY KLEINSTEIN
Seewis Dof, Switzerland

*When one lives in a region with many
old ruined castles and is familiar with
their stories from childhood, the need
eventually arises to express all of this
in terms of quilts. Thick walls, small
windows and constant remodeling in
different sections of the wall reveal their
stories. I try to reproduce these stories,
told in fragments, in my wall quilts.*

EXPANSION

Recycled cotton, silk and synthetic
fabric, metallic thread;
fused, free-motion machine quilted;
55 x 35 inches (140 x 89 cm)

MAYA CHAIMOVICH
Ramat Gan, Israel

*Every single color is a world of its own—
complete in itself. In this work, I show the
power and beauty of the combination of
colors. As in all my works, I used recycled
fabric because I like the meaning and
uniqueness of this type of fabric. I don't
know when the fabric was worn in the
past, or by whom, but I give it a new
story in my quilt.*

TROPICAL SNOWBALL

Cotton and cotton blends, Thermore
batting, cotton backing, cotton/poly threads,
bugs from photo transfers; wholecloth
reverse appliquéd, leaf enlarged from
copy of a natural specimen;
51 x 48 inches (130 x 122 cm)

BARBARA W. WATLER
Hollywood, Florida, USA

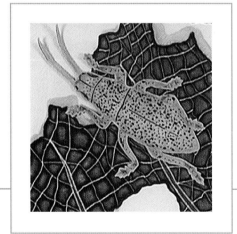

*In the tropical atmosphere of south
Florida, I am continually amazed by
the different plants and bushes that
are so plentiful in my area. The generic
name of the plant from which this
leaf was picked is "tropical snowball".
I grew up in Ohio, and found this
name, and the holes eaten by the bugs,
particularly fascinating.*

BLACK TOP

Hand-dyed/painted cotton fabrics by the
artist, some fabric discharged using bleach;
machine pieced, longarm quilted;
30 x 35 inches (76 x 89 cm)

CYNTHIA CORBIN
Woodinville, Washington, USA

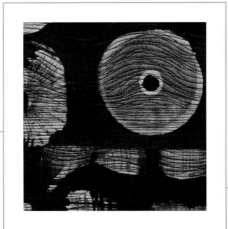

*This quilt is from a series focusing on an
anvil form. The form is upside down in
this quilt. It is the pattern in the fabric
that tells the difference between one space
and another. I love the play of marks and
texturing I can get with my approach
to dye work. I revel in accident and
experimentation. The quilt is intensively
quilted, an obsession on my part.*

SHADOW WITH
5 DIAMONDS

Hand-dyed and hand-painted cotton;
designed, pieced, appliquéd, quilted;
26 x 46 inches (66 x 117 cm)

ELIZABETH BARTON
Athens, Georgia, USA

*I hope the rhythmic relationships
between the exterior beams, outlines
and rooflines of the buildings stir
up both visual dynamics and
metaphorical musings.*

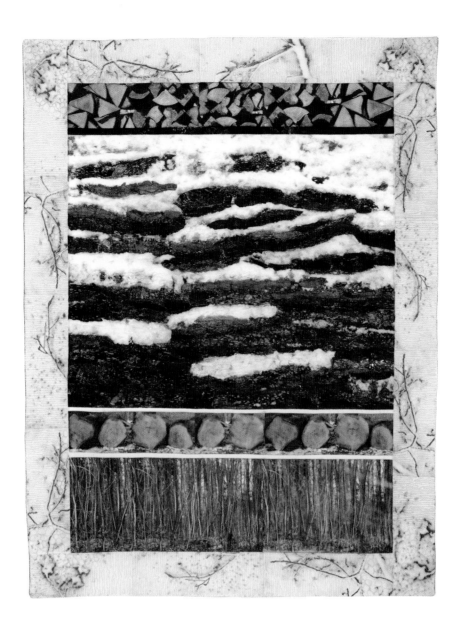

HIBERNATION

Cotton, nylon chiffon, tulle, yarn, acrylic paint, digitally processed photos; heat treated, hand embroidered, machine quilted; 34 x 45 inches (86 x 115 cm)

GRIETJE VAN DER VEEN
Oberwil, Switzerland

Fossil energy will not last forever. There is not much productive reaction to this issue. Sleep on, human being, sleep on. Responses to the natural and political environment characterize my work. Trees, flowers, rocks and water are recurring themes. I am inspired by universal organic forms and their visual aspects. Color, shape, texture and stitching are used to express my feelings.

ALLEGRETTO

Cottons and blends, Ultrasuede, wool
batting; turned-edge machine appliquéd,
machine quilted, painted;
37 x 72 inches (94 x 183 cm)

KATIE PASQUINI MASOPUST
Santa Fe, New Mexico, USA

*I make quilts from many inspirations.
Lately, I am creating quilts from paintings.
I take a small portion of a painting, and
make a drawing that is enlarged for the
templates. I create paintlike pieces so they
look as if they have been painted with a
very large brush. In reality they are all
turned-edge pieces. I then quilt them to
add even more texture.*

STRUCTURES #98

Cotton fabric, dyes, cotton batting, cotton thread; dyed, freehand designed, cut without templates or rulers, constructed and surface stitched on a home sewing machine; 30 x 29 inches (76 x 74 cm)

LISA CALL
Denver, Colorado, USA

This series originated as an exploration of human-made containment structures such as fences and stone walls. Lines of posts, negative space between stones and uniform brick rows were all of interest. As the series matured, the focus shifted to the psychological barriers we use to protect ourselves emotionally, exploring how we hide our true thoughts and feelings with these imagined roadblocks.

LADY LUCK

Recycled and commercial fabrics, found
objects; raw-edge and big-stitch hand
appliquéd, machine quilted, embellished;
27 x 37 inches (66 x 94 cm)

PAMELA ALLEN
Kingston, Ontario, Canada

*This is a good example of my sometimes
over-the-top quilting. I was experimenting
with double batting and a false trapunto
effect. It was fun "drawing" the roulette
wheel, slot machine and lucky symbols.
Of course, she has dice for hair and her
fingers are crossed!*

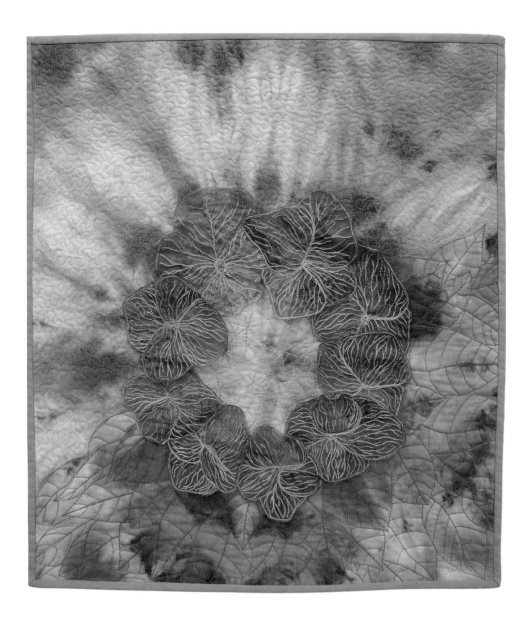

HORTENSIA

Hand-dyed cotton, organdy, yarn;
machine embroidered, machine quilted;
21 x 24 inches (54 x 61 cm)

RITA BERGHUIS-ENSING
Groningen, The Netherlands

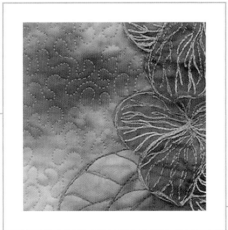

*I am fascinated by light and color. I love to
explore textiles and textile-like materials.
In my work, I use the endless possibilities
of changing the texture by stitching,
dyeing, cutting, tearing, rearranging and
embellishing to tell my stories. I find
inspiration in culture and nature, but also
in everyday life. I work spontaneously,
intuitively, striving for a perfect color
balance and for subtle contrasts in color.*

LEFT TURN
LANE #19

Peruvian pima cotton sateen, wholecloth,
fiber-reactive dyes, hand-dyed cotton
muslin, 80-percent cotton batting, cotton,
rayon, metallic thread; machine quilted;
51 x 77 inches (130 x 196 cm)

THELMA SMITH
Ventura, California, USA

*Trudging up from the Greyhound
station, downtown Tucson, among the
high rises. There strides a man out of
place and out of sync with the world
he is passing through. He walks with
purpose, turning the corner and out of
sight. What is that heavy old raincoat
doing in downtown Tucson on a summer
day with 10-percent humidity?*

THE PROMISING FRUIT

Cotton fabric, some hand-dyed by the artist,
fibers; machine appliquéd, machine quilted;
about 60 x 60 inches (150 x 150 cm)

NAVAH LIBERMAN
Ra'anana, Israel

*I love pomegranates for their vibrant color
and distinctive shape. They symbolize
something that is whole and complete.
All of the red parts in this quilt are made
from diverse fibers, treated using a variety
of techniques. The quilt is not a perfect
square, and several leaves poke out on
every side. This mimics a tree, in which
the leaves burst out wherever they choose.*

CHAIN OF RINGS

Hand-dyed and commercial cotton fabric;
machine stitched, machine quilted;
47 x 32 inches (120 x 80 cm)

AMIRA WISHINSKY
Tel Aviv, Israel

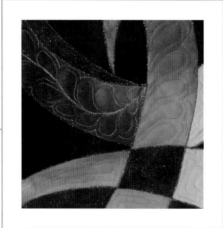

*This piece is made from a variety of
fabrics, including hand-dyed fabrics
from artists Judy Robertson and
Melody Johnson, as well as commercial
fabrics. The backing is cotton and the
middle is fusible backing. The piece was
designed for a quilting exhibit called
"We Won't Stop Singing."*

STEP-BY-STEP: INTERCONNECTING SHAPES

In *Chain of Rings* (opposite page), interconnecting shapes are sketched and numbered on paper before being traced onto web-backed fabric. After the fabric shapes are cut, they are reassembled on the cotton and sewn into place.

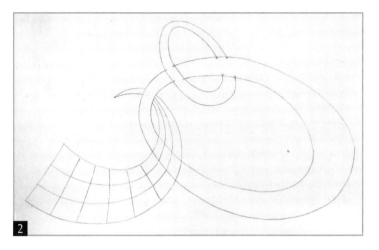

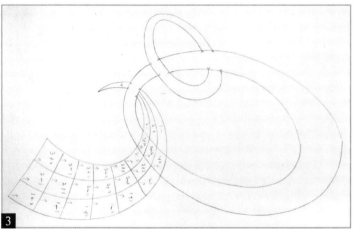

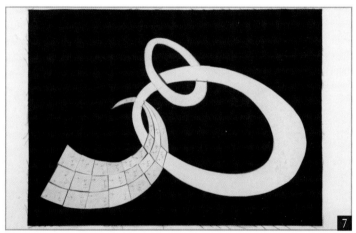

1. Select the fabric for your quilt.

2. Sketch the quilt design on white paper, then copy it onto freezer paper.

3. Mark the meeting points between the various pieces, then cut out the freezer paper.

4. Iron fusible web backing onto the wrong side of the fabric pieces, then iron the freezer paper onto the web-backed pieces of fabric.

5. Cut the fabric.

6. Remove the freezer paper from each piece of fabric, leaving behind just the fusible web.

7. Position the fabric pieces on the cotton top and iron into place.

8. Remove the freezer paper from the front of the fabric pieces.

9. Sew around each piece of fabric several times, connecting the pieces.

10. Lay the quilt lining on your work surface. Top with acrylic filler and the top layer.

11. Finish the quilt with free-motion machine quilting, using stitches that complement the shapes on the quilt. ■

I SPY

Commercial cotton, wool, cotton and
cotton-blend thread, vintage bone button;
machine and hand appliquéd, machine
quilted, handstitched;
14 x 14 inches (36 x 36 cm)

LORA A. ROCKE
Lincoln, Nebraska, USA

*When I was a little girl, cameras were
very simple and shot only black-and-white
pictures. Known as Brownie cameras, they
were small, square, difficult to aim, and it
took some time to locate the subject in the
viewfinder. This little boy's mother kept
saying, "I spy a little boy," to keep him
looking at the camera. In response, he put
his fingers to his eye and said, "I spy!"*

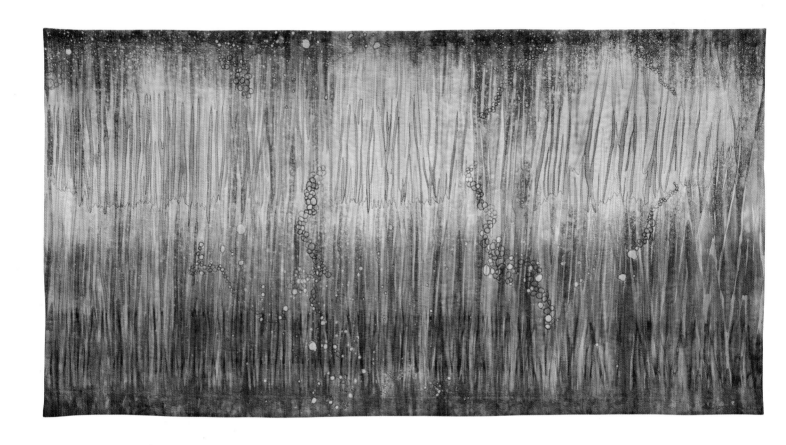

JULY

Commercially dyed cotton, discharged
and over-dyed several times, cotton and
rayon thread; pole wrapped, discharged,
dyed several times, quilted;
42 x 22 inches (107 x 56 cm)

DEBORAH GREGORY
Bellevue, Washington, USA

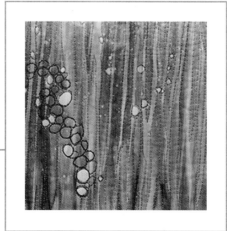

*This is a celebratory work. Its yellow
and gold colors reflect the warmth of the
month of July and its bright vegetation.
It is part of a series visually describing
the change of seasons as we move
through the calendar year.*

DRESS NIKE ALL ALONE

Cotton, tulle, translucent organdy;
quilted, burned, digital and
free-motion machine embroidered;
56 x 21 inches (142 x 54 cm)

CHARLOTTE YDE
Frederiksberg, Denmark

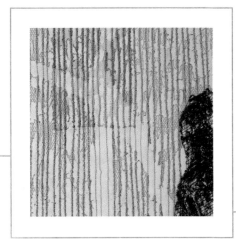

When I was young, I studied Old Greek and Latin and learned to love the art from that period. To me, it represents the roots of our democratic culture in Europe. I have a great fondness for fabric and folds, and many old statues depict folded textiles in a magnificent way. This quilt features a rough-stitched-sketchlike representation of Nike, the Goddess of Victory.

HARMONY

Hand-dyed and commercial cotton and other
fabrics; appliquéd and machine quilted;
39 x 62 inches (98 x 159 cm)

ELS VEREYCKEN
Hasselt, Belgium

*As a child, I often saw my mother
making and designing hats and clothes.
I initially trained as a biology teacher;
after I retired, I threw all of my energy
into the combination of drawing, painting,
designing and sewing. At first, nature was
my source of inspiration. Later on, I found
inspiration from other things as well.*

ODA PAGODA

Commercial cotton fabrics, acrylic beads, glass beads, cotton embroidery floss, recycled chopsticks, synthetic felt backing; fused raw edge appliquéd, freeform embroidered, machine quilted, machine stitched, burnt, wrapped with embroidery floss;
15 x 12 inches (38 x 30 cm)

JANICE PAINE-DAWES
Lakeview, Arkansas, USA

I come from a 2-D background. Sometimes organic shapes fit a composition by letting it flow until it says that it is finished. That is difficult to do when painting on paper or canvas. My quilts use fabric instead of paint and evolve from my continual exploration of form and color by letting the art determine the finished size and shaped edge of the artwork.

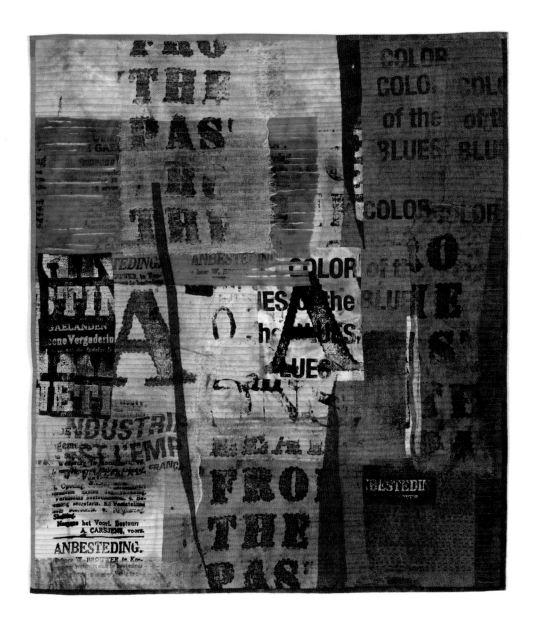

TOWNSCAPE 2

Cotton, cheesecloth, organdy; screen
printed, rusted, slashed, collaged, hand
and machine quilted;
30 x 34 inches (75 x 87 cm)

JETTE CLOVER
Antwerp, Belgium

*I am drawn to surfaces that show signs
of age, such as peeling paint, rusted
metal, worn word and torn paper.
I used to be a journalist, so language
and communication are important to me.
Letters and words are always present in
my works. I am inspired by city walls,
where fragmented, overlapping and torn
posters and advertisements compete with
graffiti for your attention.*

FLORI FLORA #7

Artist-dyed cotton batiste, sheer fabric,
cotton batting, beads; stamped with
self-made stamps, photo transferred,
machine quilted, double sided;
40 x 40 inches (102 x 102 cm)

LUTGARD GERBER-BILLIAU
Grimbergen, Belgium

*What I like most is to be surrounded
daily by fabric, threads, the sewing
machine, the computer and paint. In the
making of art quilts, the dyed fabric is
often the starting point, the inspiration,
in combination with other materials like
plastic, voile, nonwoven fabric, etc. I use
the computer to design, but almost never
follow the pattern until the end.*

BIRD OF PARADISE

Acrylic-painted silk, painted cotton;
layered, machine constructed,
machine quilted;
69 x 46 inches (175 x 117 cm)

NELDA WARKENTIN
Anchorage, Alaska, USA

*My art expresses Nature's color,
pattern, rhythm and common design
elements, such as the arc and curved
line. Constructing the quilt in sections
adds interest, as the curved imagery
contrasts with the straight line where the
sections connect. My goal is to enrich the
viewer's life with work that is beautiful,
meaningful and captivating.*

BONGWEFELA

Hand-dyed string and cotton fabric, beads;
machine appliquéd, hand quilted;
65 x 88 inches (165 x 223 cm)

SALLY SCOTT
Grahamstown, South Africa

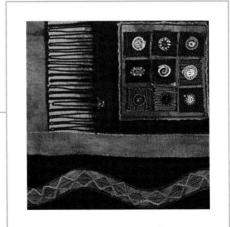

Bongwefela *means unity. It is a
celebration of life, love and the power
of the human spirit. This quilt seeks
to capture the energy and vibration of
the life force, that elusive quality that
unites us all. It alludes to transitions and
moving between worlds, both physical
and spiritual, and is my prayer for peace,
tolerance, compassion and understanding
amongst all the nations of the world.*

SLEEP

Canvas, acrylic paint, image transfers,
horsehair netting; painted, sanded,
stenciled, screen printed, machine
quilted, bound with beads;
48 x 63 inches (122 x 160 cm)

WENDY HUHN
Dexter, Oregon, USA

*I am obsessed with imagery, bright
colors and shiny things, not unlike
a crow or a small child. I always
have been. The imagery that I use is
gathered from a variety of influences
and sources, mainly from my childhood
and the possessions that surround me.
I am a visual scavenger of imagery.
My intention is to preserve these visual
metaphors and honor the source.*

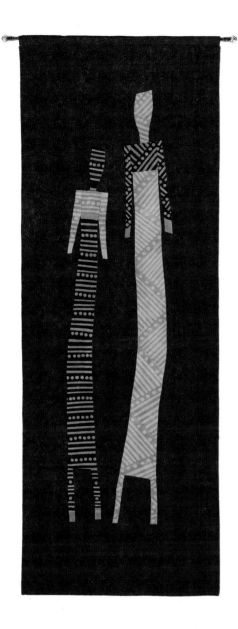
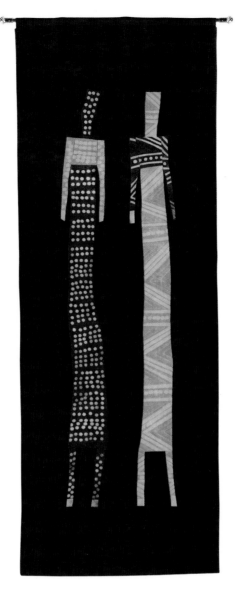
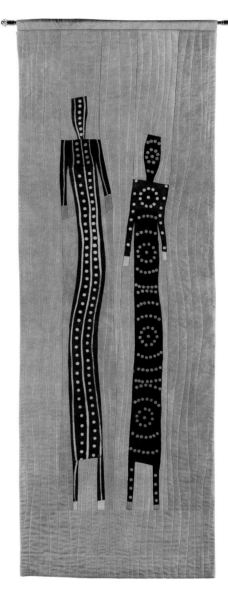

MIMI SPIRITS

Cotton sateen hand dyed and discharged by
the artist; machine pieced, machine quilted;
62 x 49 inches (157 x 124 cm)

BARBARA NEPOM
Bainbridge Island, Washington, USA

*Folklore from the indigenous people of
northern Australia describes Mimi Spirits
as fairylike beings who are so thin and
elongated that they must hide in rock
crevices during windy weather. Tall,
cylindrical sculptures and rock paintings
of these creatures seen during a trip to
Australia inspired this piece.*

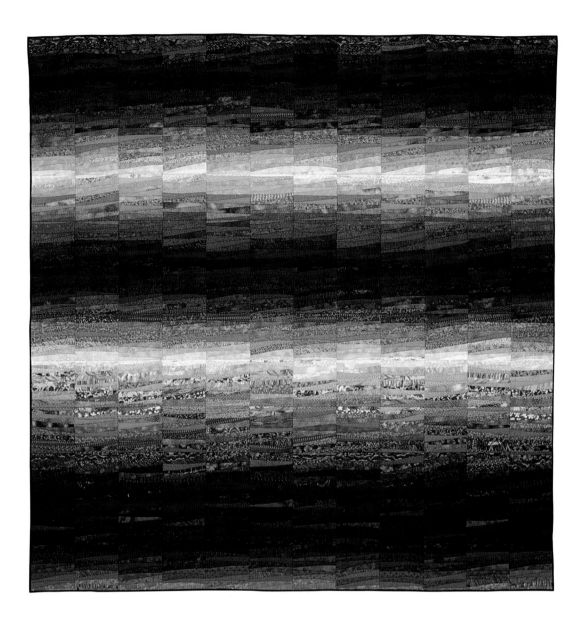

DREAMS OF THE DAWN

Cotton, cotton batting; blocks made one at a time, joined, all bindings hand finished; 96 x 96 inches (244 x 244 cm)

ANN BRAUER
Shelburne Falls, Massachusetts, USA

Growing up on a farm in the Midwest, I have always been inspired by the endless horizon of the prairies and the sweep of the sky. My quilts are abstract landscapes that capture a firm sense of the importance of place and the moment. I make the quilts one block at a time using a method I call "quilt-as-you-go."

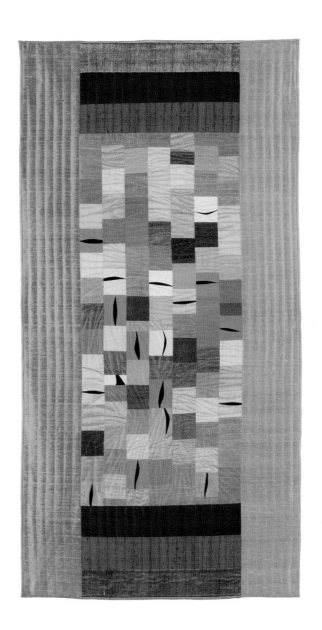

MOVEMENT IN COLOR AND MARKINGS #2

Silk, cotton fabrics, poly batting;
machine pieced, hand quilted;
24 x 46 inches (61 x 117 cm)

DAPHNE TAYLOR
New York, New York, USA

My quilts honor my love of drawing and painting. Lines reminiscent of landscape and figure are embroidered and composed within frameworks ranging from open white spaces to complex color fields. The visual language of these lines and markings is influenced and restrained by the power of simplicity.

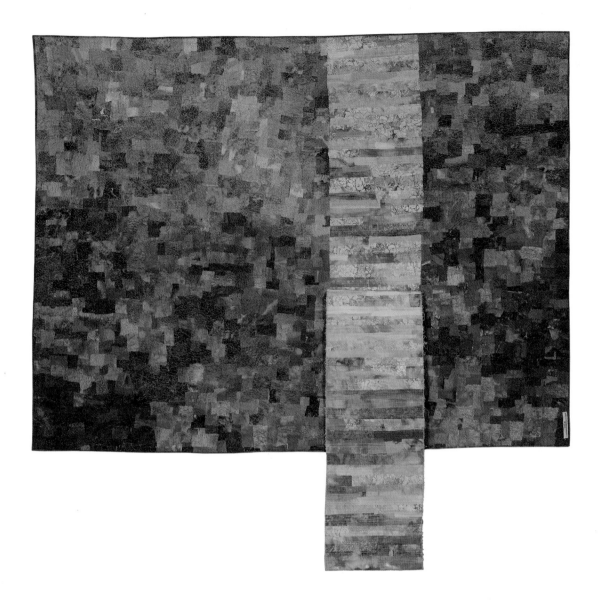

REPETITION

Cotton, silk, linen;
free machine raw appliquéd;
54 x 40 inches (137 x 102 cm)

DIRKJE VAN DER HORST-BEETSMA
Hoevelaken, The Netherlands

*In this work, it all comes together: the blue
of the water, the green of the landscape.
I have made many works with a flap.
The flap is like peeling off wallpaper and
seeing some other color surprise you.*

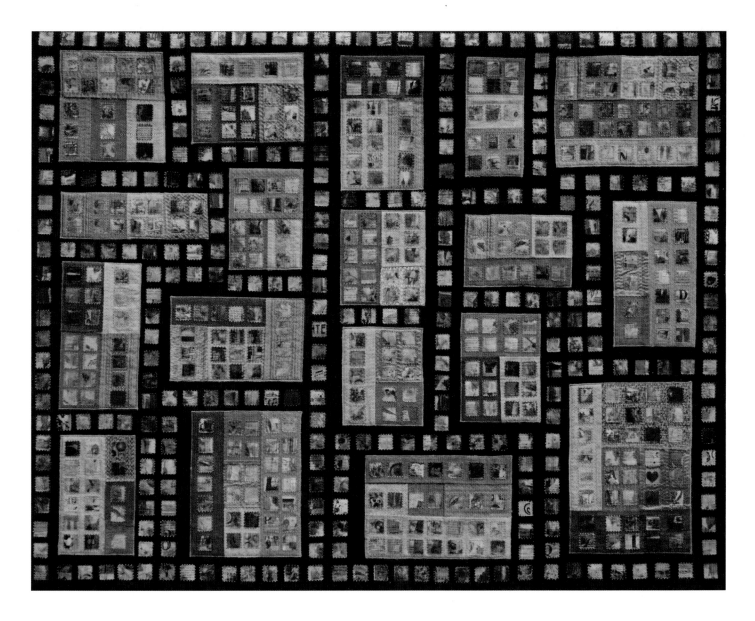

SNAPSHOTS

Black velvet, furnishing fabric, fabric, paper, size 11° seed beads; machine quilted, machine and hand appliquéd, fabric and paper collage, hand beaded; 52 x 41 inches (132 x 104 cm)

FRIEDA OXENHAM
Peeblesshire, United Kingdom

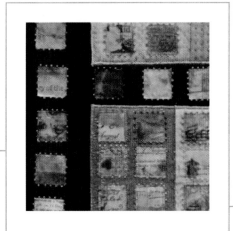

After making fabric quilts for years, I became increasingly obsessed by mixed media and started making Artist Trading Cards (ATCs) and inchies. This flowed into my quilts, and I began making collages with fabric, vintage text, images and paper napkins and cut these into 1-inch squares. In this quilt, these inchies make a view of a map or apartment building.

BLOOM

Cotton, velvet, synthetic materials,
fusible interfacing,
hand-dyed fabric;
free-motion machine quilted;
60 x 79 inches (153 x 200 cm)

MAYA CHAIMOVICH
Ramat Gan, Israel

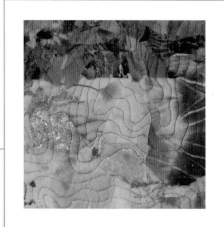

*The first inklings of this quilt came as
I was completing a previous work—
that's how it often is with my work. I
usually start with a general idea and a
sense of color. The idea of the final piece
becomes clearer over time, but I never
draw a pattern or plan. Instead, I allow
the quilt to develop as the individual
patches of fabric are sewn together.*

STEP-BY-STEP: FREEHAND FABRIC

In *Bloom* (opposite page), a wide variety of similarly colored fabrics are cut free[...] into colorful fabric blocks. These blocks are assembled using free-motion m[...]

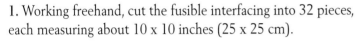

1. Working freehand, cut the fusible interfacing into 32 pieces, each measuring about 10 x 10 inches (25 x 25 cm).

2. Working freehand, cut various pieces of fuchsia fabric into strips that are about ¾ inch (2 cm) wide.

3. Lay a piece of fusible interfacing on your work surface and arrange the fabric strips on top, allowing them to overlap slightly. If you need to move the fusible interfacing before pressing the strips with an iron, place a piece of cardboard underneath the interfacing to make it easier to move.

4. When you are satisfied with the composition of the fabric, press the strips with an iron to fuse in place.

5. If some of the strips are made from synthetic material, place a piece of parchment paper under the iron to prevent the material from sticking.

7

10

8

9. Continue making fabric blocks, in various colors and shades, until you have covered all 32 pieces of fusible interfacing.

10. Arrange the fabric blocks until you are satisfied with their overall composition. This process is a bit like assembling a puzzle, only there is no incorrect combination.

11. Lay the quilt backing on your work surface and place fusible batting on top. Arrange the blocks of fabric on the batting, right side up. Allow the blocks to overlap by about ½ inch (1.3 cm) on every side so that the seams aren't visible.

12. Press the three layers together. Free-motion machine quilt the blocks into place using a variety of colored threads. ■

6. When the fabric strips are secured, turn over the interfacing and press the other side.

7. Working freehand, cut various pieces of dark green fabric into relatively large, randomly shaped pieces. Arrange the pieces on a piece of fusible interfacing, allowing them to overlap slightly.

8. Working freehand, cut various pieces of light green fabric into relatively small randomly shaped pieces. Arrange the pieces on a piece of fusible interfacing, allowing them to overlap slightly.

PASSAGEWAY
I & II

Commercial printed cottons;
machine pieced and quilted;
two pieces, each 26 x 43 inches
(66 x 109 cm)

BEATRIZ GRAYSON
Winchester, Massachusetts, USA

*The inspiration for this quilt was a photo
taken in the Jewish Quarter of the Old
City in Jerusalem. The location challenged
my mind; so many ins and outs. When I
stand about five feet from this diptych,
I feel as if I could walk right into it.*

GARRET I

Synthetic fiber, OHP (overhead
projector) sheet, canvas, silk, paper;
machine quilted, ink-jet printed,
freehand drawn, transcripted, printed,
burnt by a candle;
39 x 39 inches (99 x 99 cm)

CHIAKI DOSHO
Kawasaki-shi, Kanagawa-ken, Japan

*This Garret series is my newest collection.
It puts a photograph together with various
subject matter. I bake it and, as a last
step, take a candle to the work.*

RHAPSODY WATERSHED

Cotton, fabric paint, black netting,
various threads; painted wholecloth,
machine stitched, machine quilted;
30 x 45 inches (76 x 114 cm)

EILEEN DOUGHTY
Vienna, Virginia, USA

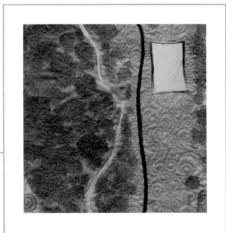

*Access to clean water is expected to
become one of the critical issues of this
century, even more important than access
to energy resources. My Watershed series
explores issues of water pollution and
erosion. This quilt, the second in the
series, depicts the waste of rainwater
in my suburban neighborhood due to
impermeable surfaces.*

WHEN BEES DISAPPEAR

Cotton, digitally printed fabric, cotton batting, metallic silver thread, beads; hand appliquéd, hand embroidered, hand quilted, machine stitched; 37 x 35 inches (93 x 88 cm)

LIN HSIN-CHEN
Tainan City, Taiwan

Nature always inspires me, especially the beauty of plants. I love to work with assorted extra print fabrics; exploring possible combinations always brings me new visions. I enjoy the journeys of making quilts. Opening my inner self to a theme can start adventures and reflection.

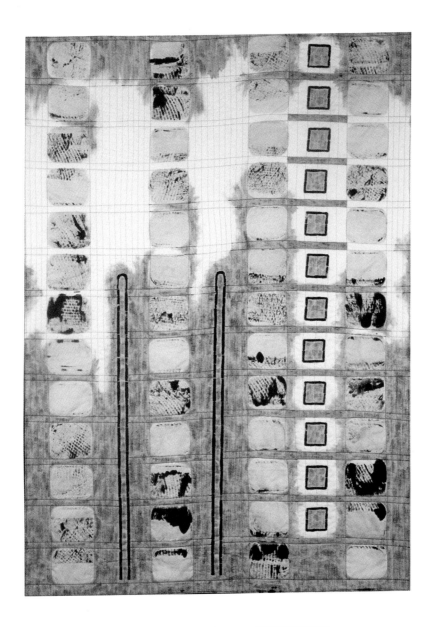

ORANGE CONSTRUCTION FENCE SERIES #62

Fabric paint, acrylic paint, thread,
cotton; monoprinted, hand painted,
machine stitched;
33 x 48 inches (84 x 122 cm)

JEANNE WILLIAMSON
Natick, Massachusetts, USA

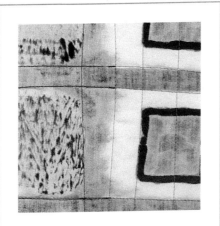

I am very interested in working with monoprints of construction fences and how they relate to nature, architecture and to other construction fence patterns.

TRINITY: JUST TELL HIM THE TRUTH

Cotton, commercial printed fabrics;
machine appliquéd, quilted, embroidered;
41 x 41 inches (104 x 104 cm)

LORI LUPE PELISH
Niskayuna, New York, USA

In a world where the truth has become hard to determine, a plea is issued. Three generations are depicted to represent us all.

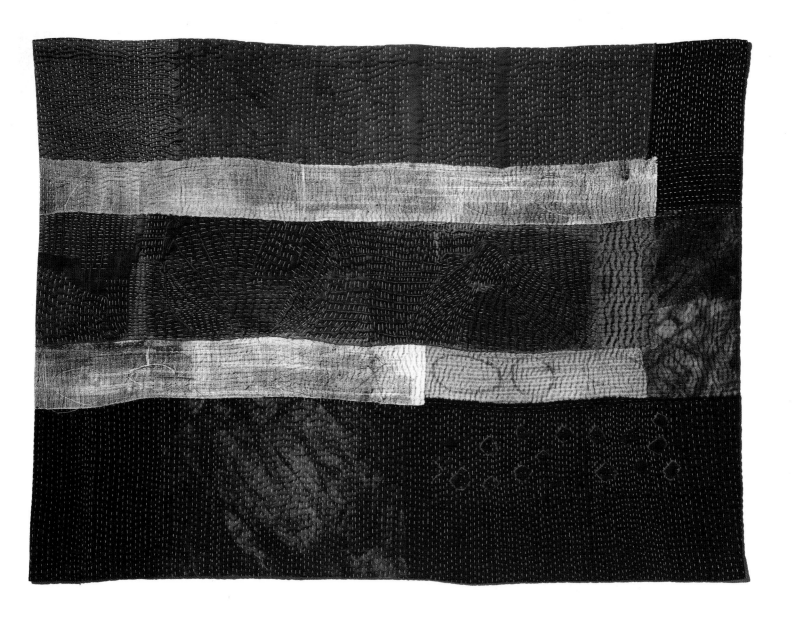

SKIN/
EUCALYPTUS

Plant-dyed silk and wool;
plant dyed, machine pieced,
handstitched, monoprinted;
40 x 29 inches (102 x 74 cm)

PAMELA FITZSIMONS
Mount Vincent, New South Wales, Australia

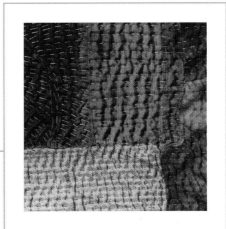

*Working with cloth is a tactile and
sensory process. The methods I employ
are simple but time consuming: collecting
plant material for dyeing, simmering
fabric for hours in a dye bath, the slow
and meditative process of handstitching.
My work is a poetic abstract response
to the landscape. Although it may seem
minimalist, on closer inspection it is
dense with stitch and meaning.*

MOYOBAMBA ORCHIDACEA

Cotton fabric, cotton batting, fabric
paint, cotton embroidery thread;
wholecloth painted, quilted,
hand embroidered;
36 x 35 inches (91 x 89 cm)

PATTY HIEB
Seattle, Washington, USA

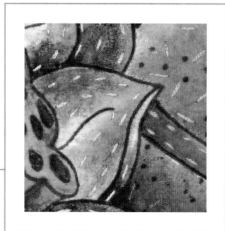

*This quilt is dedicated to the city of
Moyobamba, Peru. The city is known
also as the City of Orchids because of the
3,500 species that grow in its vicinity.*

CUP MANDALA

Fabric, thread, acrylic paint; machine pieced,
machine quilted, felt-tip-pen drawing
enlarged and printed onto cotton;
65 x 75 inches (165 x 190 cm)

THERESE MAY
San Jose, California, USA

*Each person is unique and capable
of expressing something which reflects
his/her own individual quality. There is
a Creative Spiritual Energy, which flows
through us all, and which connects us all
I believe that we can use this energy to
create whatever we want to experience in
life. My life has been transformed because
of my Creative and Spiritual practice.*

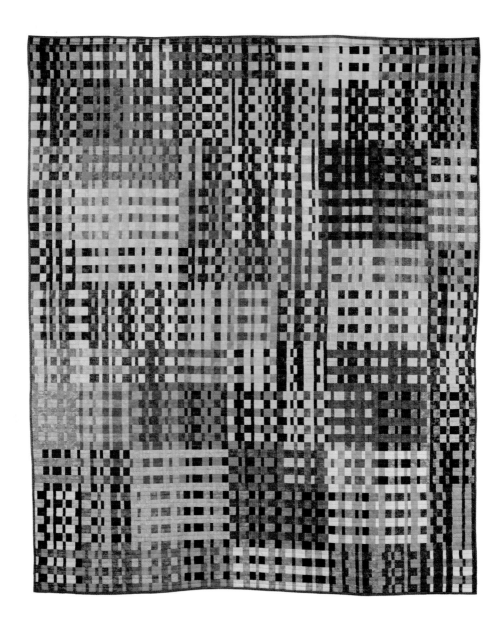

A COMPLETE
BASKET CASE

Cotton fabrics, cotton thread;
machine pieced, machine quilted;
67 x 82 inches (170 x 208 cm)

KENT WILLIAMS
Madison, Wisconsin, USA

*As a geometric abstractionist, I use
line and color to delineate shapes and
space. Sometimes, there's a strong
sense of landscape in my work—in a
very abstract way. Usually, I pursue
some kind of patterning idea, repeating
elements while varying them slightly to
create large, subtly complex compositions.
I like to form patterns that owe
something to both choice and chance.*

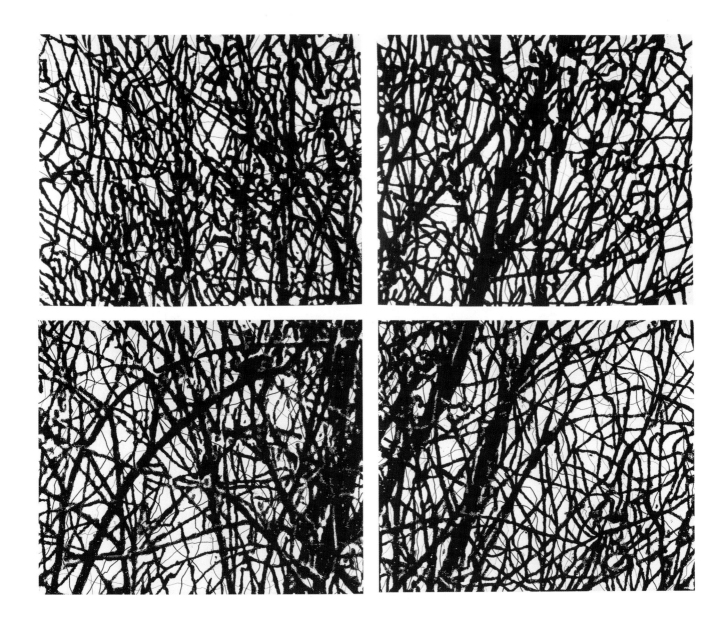

STILLNESS

Cotton/Ply blends, Thermore batting,
cotton/poly threads, cotton backing;
wholecloth reverse-appliquéd, machine
satin-stitched and embellished;
four panels, 136 x 113 inches (345 x 287 cm)

BARBARA W. WATLER
Hollywood, Florida, USA

Growing up in northeastern Ohio provided indelible memories of rural trees in wintertime. Several driving trips through Ontario, Canada, brought back childhood visions of bare trees in the landscape that follows the Still River, in the region near southeastern Georgian Bay.

BLUE OCEAN, TURQUOISE SEA

Commercial and hand-dyed cotton, silk,
silk-and-polyester organza, velvet;
overlay- and cutaway-collage appliquéd,
machine sewn, couched threads, beaded,
hand embroidered and embellished;
17 x 22 inches (43 x 56 cm)

DAPHNE GREIG
North Saanich, British Columbia, Canada

*My work is influenced by the natural
world around my home and studio in
North Saanich, British Columbia. This
world includes the Pacific Ocean. The
great oceans cover three-quarters of the
earth, regulate global temperatures, shape
weather patterns and are one of the most
important food sources for millions of
people. We must protect them and pay
attention to what they are telling us.*

LOOKING OUT THE BACK

Hand-dyed and hand-painted cotton;
designed, pieced, appliquéd, quilted;
56 x 27 inches (142 x 66 cm)

ELIZABETH BARTON
Athens, Georgia, USA

*My quilts explore the beauty of
buildings and the effects of time, creating
a sense of place but also revealing the
image's dynamic bones. I want the clear
strong colors to indicate clarity, strength
and purpose. I feel we need to face
reality—no more obfuscation!*

BYPASSED

Cotton, synthetics; dyed, screen printed,
collaged, hot cut, machine quilted;
47 x 71 inches (120 x 180 cm)

ESZTER BORNEMISZA
Budapest, Hungary

*My main sources of inspiration are the
layers of history and ages in the earth,
and in our minds. Signs and traces
of the past, and their meanings for us
in the present. I like to use maps of
ancient settlements and dwellings that
preserve the spirit of people who lived
there. I apply fragments of these maps
like enigmatic signs or symbols.*

SNOW FLOWER

Cotton, mixed tissues for interior and
fashion, acetate, woolen (felted) rope,
cotton embroidery thread;
machine pieced and appliquéd,
handstitched, machine quilted;
48 x 60 inches (122 x 153 cm)

KATRIINA FLENSBURG
Storvreta, Sweden

*This quilt was a personal artistic challenge
of making a balanced composition of
some somewhat "odd" pieces of fabric and
material (such as some graphic tissues
for interior decoration, felted woolen rope,
and tissues with various consistencies for
clothing). The inspirational starting point
was a long cherished scrap of Marimekko
fabric, which I named* Snow Flower.

AND THERE WAS EVENING, AND THERE WAS MORNING...

Hand-dyed fabric, tulle, fibers, embroidery thread; dyed, machine stitched, machine quilted, hand embroidered; 22 x 22 inches (56 x 56 cm)

For this project, I dyed the fabric by hand, so the actual composition was inspired primarily by the resulting fabric. Once the fabric was ready, I thought about how the colors made me feel and what memories they evoked. This piece is part of a triptych—a single work composed of three separate sections.

NAVAH LIBERMAN
Ra'anana, Israel

STEP-BY-STEP: HAND-DYED FIBERS

Natural fibers are a soft, malleable material for embellishment. In *And There Was Evening, and There Was Morning...* (opposite page), natural fibers are dyed, embroidered and then sewn on to the quilt.

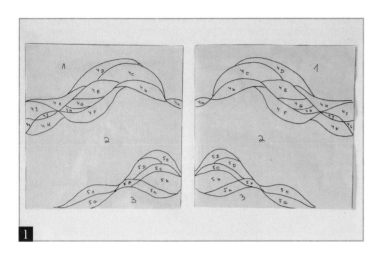

1. Sketch out a rough design of the quilt. Transfer the drawing to white paper and draw a mirror image onto paper-backed fusible web. Number each piece in the pattern, both on the white paper and the fusible web. Cut the fusible web.

2. To make the backing, lay cotton fabric on your work surface and iron on the fusible batting.

3. Starting with the largest cut pieces of fusible web, press the pieces onto the wrong side of your fabric, then cut the fabric along the edge of the pattern.

4. When all large pieces have been prepared, remove the paper from the fusible web and arrange the fabric on the batting. Use the numbers in the original drawing as a guide. Secure the pieces with headpins.

5. After the larger pieces have been cut and placed, cut the smaller pieces. To do this, press the pieces of fusible web onto the wrong side of the fabric. Add a ¼ inch (0.6 cm) margin along one side of each piece, then cut the fabric. The extra margin on each piece ensures that there aren't any spaces between the pieces when they are assembled.

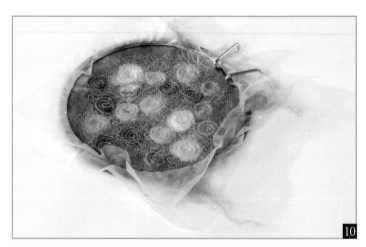

6. Arrange the smaller pieces on the batting, placing the excess margins under the adjacent pieces. When all of the pieces are in place, remove the headpins, and press the pieces with an iron.

7. Machine quilt the pieces together, sewing seams between each pieces. Add embroidered designs, as desired.

8. To prepare the fibers, select several colors of fiber, wind them into spirals and place them on a piece of water-soluble stabilizer. Place another piece of water soluble stabilizer on top, sandwiching the fibers between the two sheets.

9. Secure all three layers together by placing them inside an embroidery hoop.

10. Machine sew the fibers using decorative thread and free-motion embroidery.

11. When the fibers are secure, remove them from the embroidery hoop. Rinse in cold water for about 30 seconds, then lay on a paper tower and set aside until dry.

12. Cut the embroidered fibers as desired. Arrange them on the top of the quilt and embroider into place.

13. To add shade and shadows to the quilt, cut tulle into strips and place on fusible web. Place a piece of parchment paper on top of the tulle, then iron. Lay the tulle on top of the quilt and press into place. Machine quilt to secure. ■

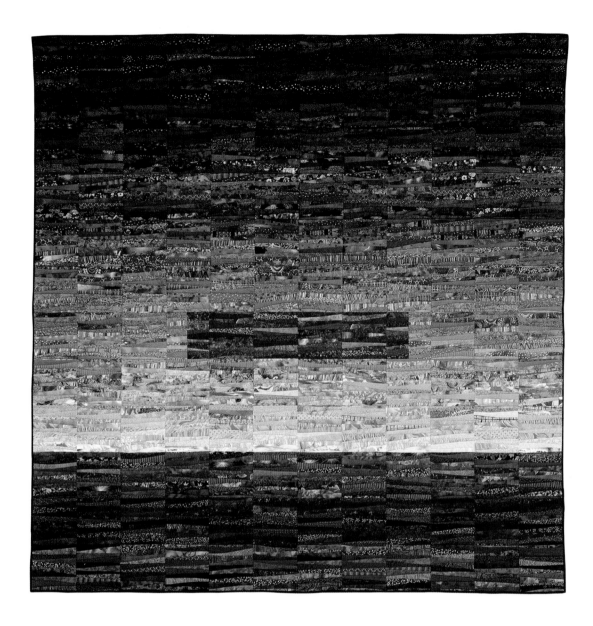

PRAIRIE DAWN

Cotton, cotton batting; joined handmade
blocks, all bindings hand finished;
96 x 96 inches (244 x 244 cm)

ANN BRAUER
Shelburne Falls, Massachusetts, USA

*I use a wide variety of colors and fabrics
to create a feeling of movement, in simple
patterns that combine to tell a story. The
intensity of the labor required to make
these quilts, the repetition of the blocks
and the wide variety of fabrics incorporate
the memories of traditional quilts and
the importance of human effort, while
reflecting contemporary life.*

FAMILY REUNION

Artist-dyed and painted cotton fabric,
batting, thread; hand dyed, deconstructed
screen printed, hand painted, monoprinted;
40 x 32 inches (102 x 81 cm)

CATHERINE KLEEMAN
Ruxton, Maryland, USA

*Vibrant colors, lavish textures and visual
depth are the hallmarks of my work.
My inspiration lies in the natural world
that surrounds me, from ocean waves
breaking on a seashore to irrigation
patterns seen from an airplane window
to the warmth of the summer sun shining
on my head. I work in abstract images
and impressions. Literal representations
seldom appear in my work.*

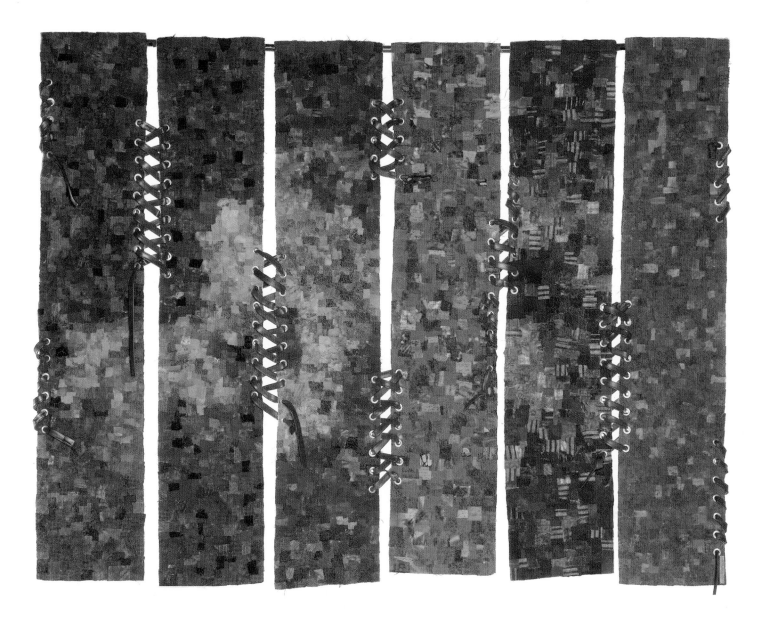

TIGHT

Cotton, silk, linen, rubber racing tire tubes;
free-machine raw appliquéd;
103 x 59 inches (262 x 176 cm)

DIRKJE VAN DER HORST-BEETSMA
Hoevelaken, The Netherlands

*To express myself, I like to work in textiles.
Maybe it is the warmth of the material,
and sometimes the memory of the textile.
It allows me to do work I like to do. In this
work, it shows freedom on the one hand
and the tightness of our "freedom" on
the other hand: work, marriage, church,
army, convention, etc.*

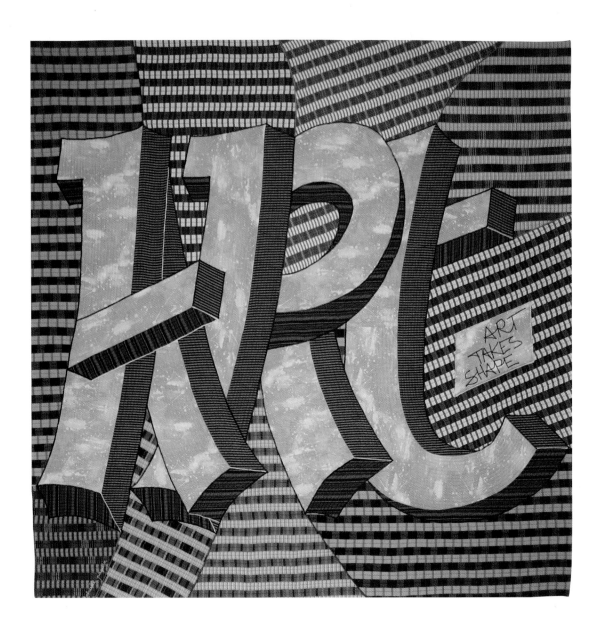

GRAFFITI

Cotton, striped fabrics; machine pieced,
machine quilted and embroidered;
51 x 51 inches (130 x 130 cm)

*My art quilts made with striped
fabrics are created for the pleasure of
experimenting with lines, colors and forms.
I like to search original designs, playing
and contrasting lines and curves.*

GABRIELLE PAQUIN
Orléans, France

IKAT KAFTAN

Indian dupion silk;
machine pieced and quilted;
64 x 49 inches (162 x 124 cm)

JUDITH ROSS
Christchurch, New Zealand

*On a visit to Istanbul I saw an
exhibition of antique Ikat: weave kaftans.
The jagged edges of the patterns have
always intrigued me. I experimented with
piecing techniques until I found a way to
suggest this aspect of Ikat weaving. This
wall hanging is one of a series of quilts
on the theme of "Traveling Cloaks," all
based on journeys I have taken.*

HOUSING DEPARTMENT #7

Hand-dyed cotton fabric and thread;
fuse appliquéd, hand embroidered,
machine quilted;
12 x 13 inches (30 x 33 cm)

LAURA WASILOWSKI
Elgin, Illinois, USA

*Colorful, hand-dyed fabrics are my
inspiration for creating art quilts, as are
stories of my family, friends and home.
I combine vivid fabrics and whimsical
stories to make pictorial quilts, which are
often narratives of my life. Each wall piece
I make is of my own design, made with
fused appliqué, hand embroidery and
machine quilting.*

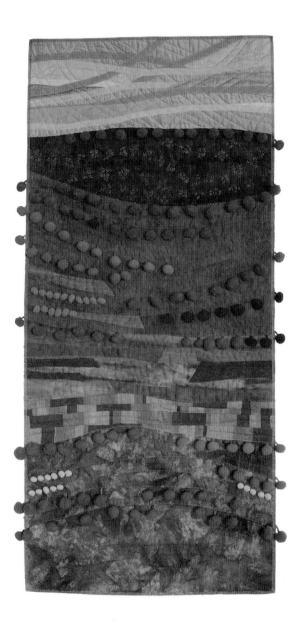

BABANANGO MEETS GREY STREET

Hand-dyed and commercial cotton fabric,
pompoms, silk organza ribbon;
hand- and machine stitched;
19 x 40 inches (48 x 102 cm)

ODETTE TOLKSDORF
Durban, South Africa

*This work is inspired from a combination
of sources: Durban's Grey Street area,
the winter landscape in rural Zululand,
pompoms that I've seen on transformed
traditional clothing, the pompom fringes
on Kuba raffia dancing skirts. I've used
pompoms in several works, and just
when I think I am finished with them,
they pull me back again.*

AT SUNRISE

Screen-printed and shibori-dyed cotton,
silk, tulle, rayon thread;
collaged, machine quilted, raw edge
quilted, machine stitched;
25 x 44 inches (64 x 112 cm)

PATTY HAWKINS
Estes Park, Colorado, USA

*I am a textile artist because I love
spontaneous dye process and exciting
results—like chocolate cake: delicious and
no calories. I am an artist because of the
lights and shadows of the day, seasons of
Aspen, amazing rock formations, skeletal
tree shapes, Colorado landscapes. Wabi
Sabi, the beauty of the imperfection in
Nature, opening viewer eyes.*

NOVEMBER STORIES

Cotton; hand- and machine stitched,
hand quilted;
33 x 22 inches (85 x 57 cm)

TRUDY KLEINSTEIN
Seewis Dof, Switzerland

*November: Wisteria leaves lie brown
and wet on the ground. Soon the snow
will come and cover them all with a
white mantle. In my mind I can still
hear their rustling and see how the wind
plays with them. The bright colors of
autumn have already departed. Now,
the color brown in all its shadings has
taken over. These are my colors. So
many ideas, so many possibilities.*

AFRO BLUE

Hand-dyed cotton fabric,
metallic thread, beads, paint;
foundation pieced, free-motion
machine quilted, hand appliquéd;
70 x 54 inches (178 x 137 cm)

MYRAH BROWN GREEN
Brooklyn, New York, USA

*My son Talu is a classically trained
musician, but his instrument of choice
is the African drum. He learned to
read music by playing the trumpet,
and graduated with a BFA in Jazz,
but his heart still is passionate about
the African drum. My son has always
loved the song "Afro Blue" written
by Mongo Santamaria, probably
because it bridges African and North
American music traditions.*

THE WRITING IS
ON THE WALL VI

Cotton, wool, silk, pigment ink;
hand dyed, hand felted, machine
stitched, handstitched;
22 x 48 inches (56 x 121 cm)

FIONA WRIGHT
Pushkar Rajasthan, India

*Interest in the natural world, travel, the
degradation of the environment and the
lack of concern for the developing world
has had great impact in recent times
on my psyche, leading to this series of
graffiti-inspired calls to action.*

SECRET DIARY 20: "GETTING ENOUGH"

Dyes on cotton; screen printed and
painted, machine pieced and quilted;
54 x 37 inches (137 x 94 cm)

ANGELA MOLL
Santa Barbara, California, USA

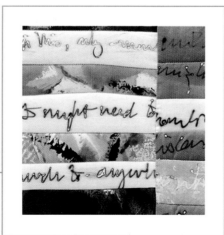

*Each quilt in the Secret Diary series is
an open notebook, the oversized text an
invitation to read. Yet the stitched diaries
are unreadable, revealing just the outline
of a life story: rhythm, pattern, layers. It
is an open book but a Secret Diary.*

CRESCENDO
(FROM THE GONG MOTIF SERIES)

Hand-dyed cotton sateen, rayon thread,
ribbon floss; quilted, stitched and couched;
67 x 86 inches (170 x 218 cm)

CAROL TAYLOR
Pittsford, New York, USA

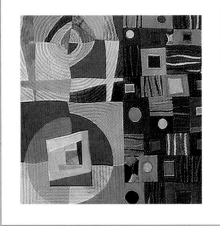

*In musical arrangements, the exciting
parts are often announced in a grand
forte after building in intensity from a
soft pianissimo. This is called a crescendo.
Like a conductor who masterfully builds
to the grand finale by punctuating notes
and tempo and by repeating rhythms,
Crescendo's subtle fabric placements,
from light to dark with interspersion of
texture, heighten the visual excitement.*

STAIRWAY TO HEAVEN

Cotton fabric, leaves, acrylic paint;
dyed and over-dyed, painted, monoprinted;
39 x 63 inches (99 x 160 cm)

ELS VEREYCKEN
Hasselt, Belgium

In quilting, nature is my most important source of inspiration. Beautifully shaped plume poppy (Macleaya cordata) leaves from my garden were used in this quilt. These summer plant leaves inspire me. They are present in some of my quilts, in a range of sizes and treated with various techniques. The leaves composed as consecutive steps visualize the concept of a staircase…to heaven.

99

ACOMA SUNSET

Artist-dyed cotton; machine
pieced and quilted;
53 x 30 inches (135 x 76 cm)

GRETCHEN B. HILL
Longmont, Colorado, USA

*Nature is the inspiration for many of
my quilts. Acoma Sunset is part of my
sunrise/sunset series. It was designed after
a visit to Albuquerque, New Mexico.
Late in the afternoon, I visited a Native
American pueblo, Acoma, to observe the
beautiful sunset. There were kiva ladders
on most of the dwellings. I loved the
different sizes and shapes of these ladders
and incorporated them in this quilt.*

ORANGE CONSTRUCTION FENCE SERIES #61

Fabric paint, acrylic paint, thread, cotton;
monoprinted, hand painted,
machine stitched;
33 x 48 inches (84 x 122 cm)

JEANNE WILLIAMSON
Natick, Massachusetts, USA

This is an abstract view of a building under construction. I combine printmaking, painting and stitching in my artwork.

LIFE AND COLOR

Hand-dyed and commercial cotton
and silk fabric; inkjet printed, machine
stitched, machine quilted;
32 x 40 inches (81 cm x 100 cm)

BELLA KAPLAN
Kfar Giladi, Israel

*This art quilt tells the story of a city
that lives under the constant threat and
reality of war. It shows how life returns
to normal, full of color and vivacity,
as soon as the bombs stop falling. The
market opens and people go back to
their daily routine.*

STEP-BY-STEP: COLOR PHOTOGRAPHS

In *Life and Color* (opposite page) digital photographs are printed on cotton fabric using a standard home printer. These fabric photos are integrated into the quilt like ordinary fabric pieces.

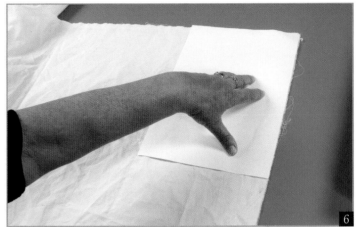

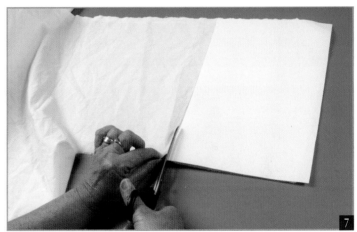

1. Photograph the objects you want to use in your quilt using a digital camera.

2. Download the photos onto a computer and select the ones you want for the quilt.

3. Select the fabrics that you'll use for the background of the quilt and the background for the photographs.

4. Dye the fabrics as desired, then set aside until dry.

5. Place a piece of printer paper on top of a piece of freezer paper and trace. Cut the freezer paper so that it is the same size as the printer paper.

6. Place a piece of printer paper on top of a piece of fabric and trace.

7. Cut the fabric so that it is ¼ inch (0.6 cm) smaller all around. (Do this so that the fabric threads don't get caught in the printer mechanism.)

8. Place the fabric on the smooth side of the freezer paper and press with an iron.

9. Insert the freezer paper-lined fabric into an inkjet printer. Make sure the fabric is oriented so that the image will be printed on the fabric (not the freezer paper). Every printer is different, so do a test run with regular paper to make sure.

10. Print the image on the fabric, and set aside until the ink dries.

11. When ink is dry, carefully peel the fabric away from the freezer paper.

12. Integrate this fabric into your quilt design, using it as you would use regular fabric. ■

REFLECTIONS, GLASS WALLS, LA DEFENSE, PARIS, VAR. 2

Hand-dyed and over-dyed painted fabric, cotton, polyester, rayon; dyed, over-dyed, painted, fused, machine stitched; 44 x 30 inches (112 x 76 cm)

BARBARA J. SCHNEIDER
Woodstock, Illinois, USA

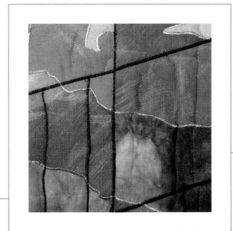

This series of art quilts is based on photos I took of glass buildings in the La Défense area of Paris, France, on a cloudy winter day. Reflection is a theme of my work. It is what I do throughout my work process, as well as what I hope viewers do as they look at the completed work.

SECRETS OF CAESTERT I

Paper, acrylic paint, cotton, interlining, lining;
machine pieced, machine embroidered,
stamped, painted, hand knotted;
43 x 43 inches (109 x 109 cm)

CHERILYN MARTIN
Nümegen, The Netherlands

*My interest in working with paper and
mixed media has led to a new body of
work in which the use of embellishment
is reduced to a minimum in order to
maximize the impact of the surface. In
this quilt, weathered surfaces bearing
intriguing marks left by man offer a
wealth of inspiration for my own mark
making in paper, paint and stitch.*

106

SYDNEY TURRET CORAL

Commercial and hand-dyed fabric;
fuse appliquéd, machine quilted;
47 x 39 inches (119 x 99 cm)

BETH MILLER
Kambah, Australia

*Coral on the ocean floor. At night, the
brilliant fragile fingers of the turret coral
probe their surroundings for waterborne
delicacies. Although flowerlike, these coral
polyps are actually animals.*

METAMORPHOSIS IN 5 DIMENSIONS

Cotton, striped fabrics; machine pieced,
machine quilted, appliquéd, embroidered;
51 x 51 inches (130 x 130 cm)

GABRIELLE PAQUIN
Orléans, France

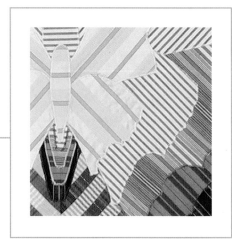

*After studying drawing and painting in
art school for several years, I decided
to use fabrics instead of oil painting.
My background in traditional quilting
helps me in this domain.*

BLUE MOON

Acrylic paint, screen print, ink, silk noil;
painted, screen printed, machine stitched,
handstitched; two pieces,
each 23 x 51 inches (58 x 129 cm)

KATHERINE K. ALLEN
Fort Lauderdale, Florida, USA

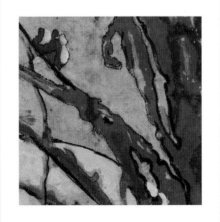

*My art is a meditation on Nature. From
garden, wetlands and woods, I gather
the raw materials I use to create my Soft
Paintings. These marks made by my hand,
brush and stitch interweave with natural
shapes from the earth to communicate
an important philosophy of coexistence in
harmony with nature. My goal is to create
an evocative artwork that nourishes mind,
eye and spirit in equal measure.*

EZEKIEL'S WHEELS

Silk, merino wool, felt batting, cotton back, silk and cotton threads; hand painted, hand appliquéd, extensively handstitched; 53 x 53 inches (135 x 135 cm)

MARIANNE BURR
Coupeville, Washington, USA

The Prophet Ezekiel had a vision of wheels in the air. Painting silk and heavily stitching it by hand combines favorite activities. I like the challenge of working on a design with additional paints and various threads to create an extremely rich surface. The work combines the wisdom of the head with the wisdom of the hands. In a world of hurry and stress this work is slow and carefully considered.

IN MY AKUABAA FORM

Cotton fabric, novelty threads, cowry shells;
free motion machine quilted, machine
appliquéd, fabric strip weaving, embellished;
80 x 95 inches (203 x 241 cm)

MYRAH BROWN GREEN
Brooklyn, New York, USA

*This quilt is my representation of the
Akubaa symbol indigenous to the
Ashanti people of Ghana, West Africa.
The symbol is a fertility symbol that
is used to keep women safe during
the childbearing months. I collect the
Akuabaa symbols and enjoy uncovering
those that I have never seen before.*

SIBYL'S SONG

Commercially printed fabric, quilting
fabric, interior decorating fabric;
machine pieced, machine quilted;
40 x 56 inches (102 x 142 cm)

SYLVIA H. EINSTEIN
Belmont, Massachusetts, USA

*This quilt is a modern version of the
Drunkard's Path pattern. The circles
move in and out of the background and
float diagonally over the surface. I love
the grid, the block and the challenge of
visually breaking the seamlines. I consider
my work a dialogue with material.*

KING SOLOMON'S MAGICAL CARPET

Hand-dyed and commercial cottons, beads, embroidery threads, machine appliquéd and pieced, hand appliquéd, hand and machine quilted, hand embroidered and beaded; 40 x 54 inches (102 x 137 cm)

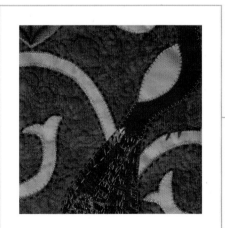

According to legend, the Queen of Sheba gave King Solomon a magical carpet. My very liberal interpretation involves much later symbolism mixing Islamic and Jewish influences.

SHULAMIT RON
Kadima, Israel

IRIS

Hand-dyed silk, batting, solid and patterned
black commercial fabric; torn, collaged,
hand cut, fused, machine quilted;
60 x 72 inches (152 x 183 cm)

MAGGIE WEISS
Evanston, Illinois, USA

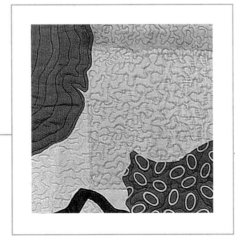

*Creating the illusion of three
dimensions on a two-dimensional
surface is a profoundly captivating
process. Close examination of natural
forms and their colors, edges, shapes
and outlines is a satisfying and joyful
part of my intuitive collage method.*

QUELLE

White cotton satin; echo quilted by hand;
83 x 83 inches (211 x 211 cm)

ADELHEID GUBSER
Cornol, Switzerland

*When working with textile, I consider
how many hands are needed to make it,
from harvesting in the fields or cocoons,
through processing, until the fabric
is ready to use. If I use new fabric, I
combine it with other fabric, giving the
fabric a second life and respecting all of
the work people put into it.*

GOLDFISH

Cotton; machine sewn, longarm quilted;
55½ x 69 inches (141 x 175 cm)

BERNADETTE MAYR
Kempten, Germany

*While a school of goldfish is swimming
in one direction in fine unity, a group of
opportunists are heading in the opposite
direction. Each fish has a different form,
a result of free-cutting technique. So
the swarm seems to move in a lively,
animated manner. The wavy quilting
emphasizes the movement of the fish.
Don't go with the flow.*

LIGHT & DARK II

Old Japanese silk kimono;
direct appliquéd, machine quilted;
two pieces, each 12 x 59 inches
(30 x 150 cm)

CHIAKI DOSHO
Kawasaki-shi, Kanagawa-ken, Japan

*I studied haute couture and sewing
when I was young, wanting to be a
designer. I made my first quilt 22 years
ago. Three years later, I made my first
art quilt. Several years later, I went
to university to learn art and textile.
Triggered by this, something changed in
me. I make works for myself now.*

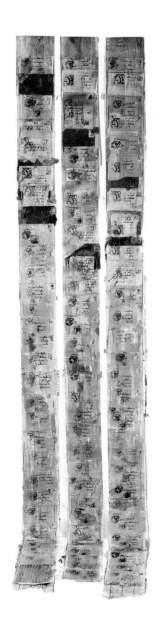

PLINIUS III IV V

Cotton, silk, paper; batiked, silkscreened,
stitched, dyed;
three pieces, each 16 x 57 inches
(40 x 145 cm)

ELS VAN BAARLE
Dreischor, The Netherlands

*Remains of structures ravaged by wind
and weather offer compelling observations.
On the surface, we discern subtle colors
and textures. This correlates to my
technique of layering wax and dyes, paper
and threads. As an old wall reveals a
treasure of details when closely observed,
so does my cloth. What appears to be one
color at first glance becomes a layer of
nuances when studied.*

THE FOREST

Commercial fabric, poly batting;
hand pieced, hand quilted;
122 x 142 inches (310 x 360 cm)

LIN HSIN-CHEN
Tainan City, Taiwan

*Nature always inspires me, especially
the beauty of plants. I love to work
with assorted print fabrics. Exploring
possibilities of combination always brings
me new visions. I enjoy the journey of
making quilts. Opening my inner self
to a theme can start adventures and
reflection. Sewing my thoughts and
feelings into fabrics strengthens a quilt's
power of conversation.*

AMPHORAE #1

Commercial and hand-dyed cotton fabric,
oil-based paint sticks, cotton and synthetic
thread, buttons, beads, cotton batting;
painted, machine quilted,
hand embroidered;
24 x 32 inches (60 x 81 cm)

SHULAMIT RON
Kadima, Israel

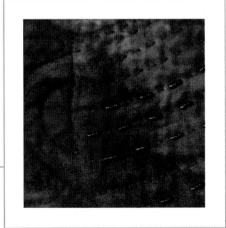

*I have been always fascinated by
archaeological artifacts, especially with
the beautiful shapes of amphorae and
pottery. This composition is a tribute to
the beauty of these shapes. The technique
combines traditional patchwork
with innovative fabric stenciling. The
stenciling creates a semi-transparent,
ethereal effect that reflects the fragility of
ancient artifacts in a different way.*

STEP-BY-STEP: OIL-BASED PAINTING

The quilt acts like a canvas for painting in *Amphorae #1* (opposite page). Handmade templates are used to trace images with oil-based paint sticks. These images are embellished using beads, buttons and decorative thread.

1. Draw, paint or sketch your quilt composition.

2. Select the fabric for your quilt.

3. Draw pottery shapes on the dull side of freezer paper. For symmetrical shapes, fold the paper in half and sketch half of it. Cut out the shapes to make templates.

4. Place a piece of fabric on your work surface and place a template on top, smooth side down. Iron the template onto the fabric.

5. Draw a thick line with the paint stick along the contoured edge of the template. Using a toothbrush, pull the paint onto the fabric.

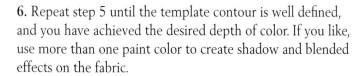

6. Repeat step 5 until the template contour is well defined, and you have achieved the desired depth of color. If you like, use more than one paint color to create shadow and blended effects on the fabric.

7. Remove the template from the fabric. Add overlapping shapes with different colors, if you like. Let the painted fabric dry for about 24 hours, then fix the oil paint by ironing.

8. Repeat steps 4 to 7 with the other templates and fabric pieces. Make a quilt sandwich by layering the painted fabric onto the batting and backing.

9. Now the fun begins. Select beads, buttons and embroidery threads in matching or contrasting colors.

10. Thread an embroidery needle and bury the knot in the batting layer.

11. Make a stitch, then string 1 to 3 beads onto the needle.

12. Make another stitch, pulling the thread to secure the beads. Repeat steps 11 and 12 to complete the design. ∎

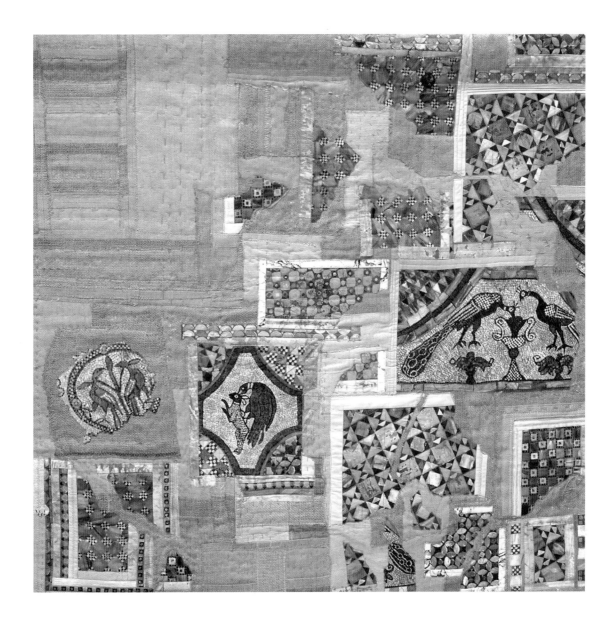

FRAGMENTS

Hessian, cotton, string, hand-printed cotton
with mosaic designs; batik and hand-printed
mosaic motifs with hand-stab quilting string;
51 x 50 inches (131 x 127 cm)

BARBARA RICHARDS
Stresa, Italy

*My quilts are inspired principally by
nature, which offers endless possibilities
of textures and structures; music,
which I like to render in a visual way;
and ancient art, which I reinterpret
in a personal way. I am particularly
stimulated to use holographic fabrics,
threads and metalized fabrics, and
I sometimes incorporate nontextile
materials in the work.*

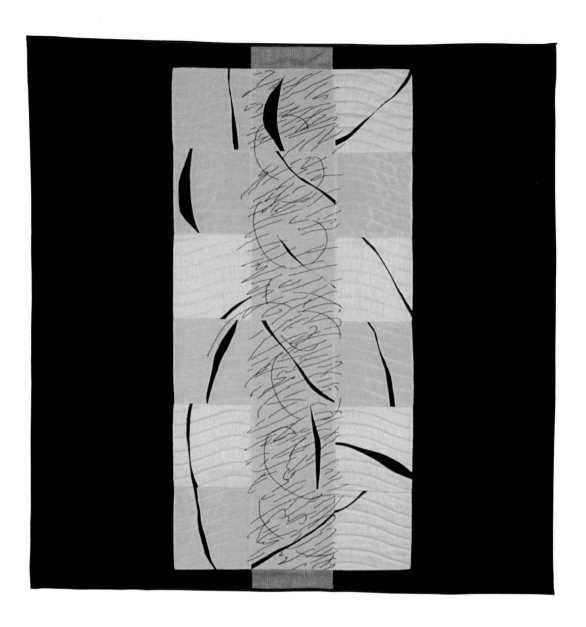

COMPOSITION IN MARKINGS AND MOVEMENT

Silk, cotton fabrics, embroidery floss,
poly batting; hand embroidered,
machine pieced, hand quilted;
36 x 36 inches (91 x 91 cm)

DAPHNE TAYLOR
New York, New York, USA

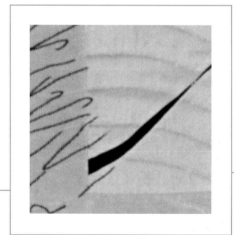

*Hand quilting is of great importance,
as it is equivalent to the act of drawing.
While the placements of the fabrics are
composed geometrically, the quilting on
top is a loose, spontaneous act. My hand
responds to the shapes in the cloth,
creating a shadow line that is simple,
clear and meditative.*

SYDNEY SEABREEZE

Hand-dyed, hand-painted, and
commercial cotton fabric;
fuse appliquéd, machine quilted;
79 x 79 inches (200 x 200 cm)

BETH MILLER
Kambah, Australia

*Sydney harbor is Australia's busiest and
most beautiful harbor. The vast flotillas of
pleasure yachts that take to the water at
every opportunity compete with the ferries
and supertankers to create pathways
across the harbor in a hive of activity.*

VENETIAN FLOTSAM

Linen, cotton, scrim, antique linen;
dyed, bleached, appliquéd, machine
and handstitched;
61 x 61 inches (155 x 155 cm)

FENELLA DAVIES
Bath, United Kingdom

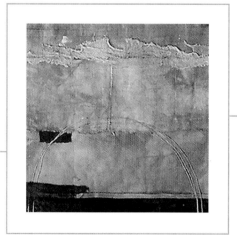

*This quilt is inspired by a visit to Venice,
Italy. The bright sun was shining against
the old walls, papers were flying in the
wind; reflections of the waters of the
canals against the walls of the palazzos.*

ARE WE SAFER NOW?

Cotton, dye, paint; lithocoal, monoprinted, painted, discharged cotton, machine pieced and appliquéd, hand and machine quilted; 40 x 46 inches (102 x 117 cm)

JUDITH PLOTNER
Gloversville, New York, USA

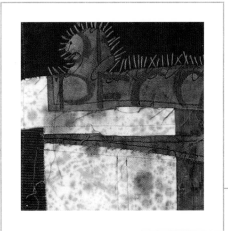

This is my response to the war in Iraq and its effect on terrorism. On monoprinted black fabric, I discharge printed text and then overprinted the names of the dead. Bright red shapes, with both type and script, portray bloody images without being graphic. Red splatters of dye and handstitching representing razor wire conveying the horrors of war.

UNLIKE HER FATHER, SHE PILES UP HER GRIEVANCES NICELY

Cotton, silk and other fabrics, batting; acrylic panel, wood box, aluminum frame; hand-dyed, machine appliquéd and quilted; 42 x 66 x 5 inches (107 x 168 x 13 cm)

I have taken a step away from figurative works to create multi-panel, conceptual pieces that allow me all sorts of freedom. I begin by slicing apart an "assembly" (sometimes a portrait that didn't work; otherwise, something I create expressly for this purpose). I then work back into the pieces with new hues and fabric.

LAUREN CAMP
Santa Fe, New Mexico, USA

L'EXISTENCE

Cotton broadcloth, silk organza;
monoprinted, painted, wax resisted,
screen printed with dye in two layers,
collaged, machine quilted;
22 x 46 inches (56 x 117 cm)

MELANIE TESTA
Brooklyn, New York, USA

*How far removed but ever so entwined
are humans from nature? Minerals,
plants and animals are not just resources;
they are fellow objects and beings in a
finite and beautiful experience called
Earth. My work seeks to reintegrate
humans, plants and animals into a
broader perception of our time here on
earth, to remove barriers and shed light
on the foundation of our existence.*

WINDOW

Cotton, low-loft batting;
deconstructed screen printed,
machine pieced, hand quilted;
17½ x 17½ inches (44 x 44 cm)

SUSAN PURNEY MARK
Victoria, British Columbia, Canada

*Fiber unites many forms and has been
an extremely important part of my life
since my earliest memories. Texture, color,
pattern and design move my inner being,
in countless ways, through my days and
nights. My journey with fabric has given
me a special sense of place. If I can move
the fabric from white to color, then I know
I am truly the creator of my work.*

KALEIDOSCOPIC XXXII: MY BROOKLYN BRIDGE

Cotton, silk; machine pieced, hand couched, longarm and hand quilted; 36 x 36 inches (91 x 91 cm)

PAULA NADELSTERN
Bronx, New York, USA

New Yorkers identify themselves by their neighborhoods. I've spent my whole life in the Bronx, but I love walking across the Brooklyn Bridge.

HIBISCUS

Acrylic paint, silk, cotton, polyester
batting, cotton backing;
painted, hand appliquéd, hand quilted;
48 x 43 inches (109 x 122 cm)

MARGARET ANDERSON
Sedona, Arizona, USA

*I approach my abstract designs
intuitively and with eager anticipation.
I love not knowing how a design will
develop until it reveals itself as I position
shapes and colors utilizing the chance
emergence of unplanned relationships. As
I spontaneously build layers of collage
my ideas become increasingly defined
until the final design emerges.*

LYELL CANYON

Silk, satin, brocade, paint;
embroidered, heat transferred, stitched;
40 x 34 inches (102 x 86 cm)

BONNIE PETERSON
Houghton, Michigan, USA

A section of California's John Muir Trail
is depicted in this piece. The borders are
embroidered with a journal entry from
The Mountains of California by John
Muir (1894): "Early next morning
I made up a bundle of bread, tied
my note-book to my belt, and strode
away in the bracing air, full of eager,
indefinite hope."

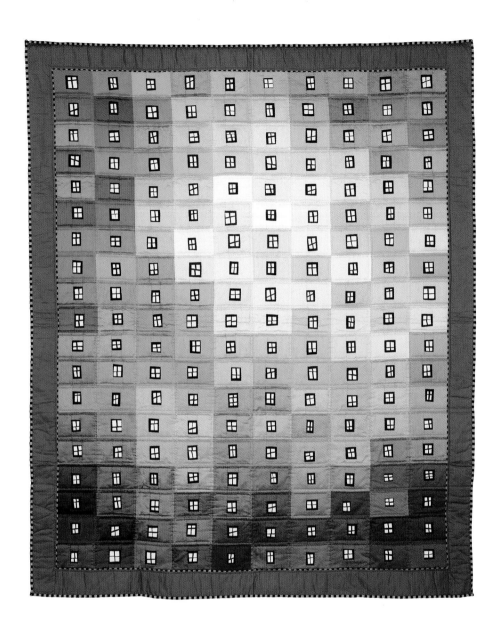

MANHATTAN

Cotton and synthetics;
machine sewn, machine quilted;
72 x 87 inches (183 x 220 cm)

BERNADETTE MAYR
Kempten, Germany

I fancy big cities. Whether it's Manhattan or another city in the world, each features its separate inhabitants. Their lives are shown by different colors and different forms of windows, even if they seem to be the same at first glance. United by the gray street, each apartment has its own light. Even the dull colors are interesting, evoked by the radiating gleam of the surrounding colors.

CARREFOUR

Hand-printed and commercial cotton fabric;
machine pieced, machine quilted;
37 x 45 inches (95 x 115 cm)

CÉCILE TRENTINI
Zurich, Switzerland

*Unlike my usual approach, this quilt was
made without any previous planning.
It was created intuitively on the design
wall, simply by listening to the fabric,
and letting it guide me. At the same time,
many experiences gained from previous
works influenced the design process. I felt
that my work was going to evolve in a
new direction, hence the title of the quilt:
Carrefour (crossroads).*

INCOMMUNICATO

Cottons, organza, textile paint;
fuse appliquéd, surface painted,
fabric manipulation, sponged;
54 x 54 inches (137 x 137 cm)

ESTERITA AUSTIN
Port Jefferson Station, New York, USA

This quilt is set at the back wall of the dining hall in a 12th century villa in Tuscany, where I teach every September. I've taken a bit of artistic license and included two people from another photo. The mobile phones are added to make a statement on how mass communication with the outside world causes personal communication to be left by the wayside.

KEYSTONE

Cotton velvet, cotton sheer, synthetic
organza; discharged, dyed, screen printed,
pieced, hot-cut, machine quilted;
35 x 59 inches (89 x 150 cm)

*My goal is to grasp bits of the mystery of
the individual and history at the same
time. By these contemplations, I try to
focus on the process of understanding
the course of time, considering these
reminiscences as part of our common
ancient knowledge.*

ESZTER BORNEMISZA
Budapest, Hungary

CHANGES II

Commercial and hand-dyed fabrics, cotton
backing, fusible batting;
machine stitched and quilted;
52 x 52 inches (132 x 132 cm)

TALLY RONLY-RIKLIS
Tel Aviv, Israel

*This quilt is about the visual effect of
graded transformation and the emotions it
arouses. I love to explore color and shade,
light and shadow, flatness and depth.
Bright strong colors inspire me, delight me
and lift my spirit. The magnificent variety
of colors and shades emerging in sunrises
and sunsets, mountains and deserts, life
under water and seasons changing are all
reflected in my works.*

STEP-BY-STEP: GRADED COLOR TRANSFORMATION

The visual effect of depth and movement in *Changes II* (opposite page) is achieved by using graded transformation of colors and shades. Thin curved strips are inserted into quilt units, and all blocks are arranged in diagonal graded color compositions.

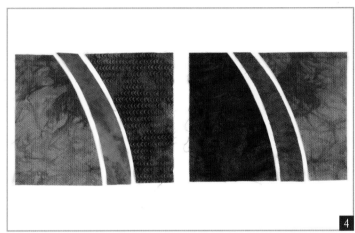

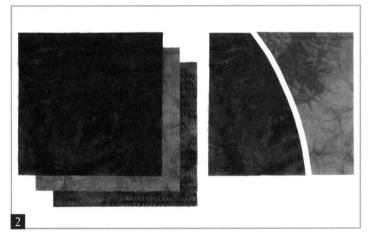

1. Select a range of fabrics, in a variety of dark, medium and light colors.

2. Cut the fabrics into 7 x 7 inch (18 x 18 cm) squares using a rotary cutter. Stack the fabric squares, right side up, in groups of three, so that each square in the stack is of a different fabric shade or color. Press the stack with an iron to prevent the fabrics from moving. Cut each stack into two sections with a curved line.

3. Make a template for a banana-shaped strip of fabric that will be inserted between the two sections of each square.

Place the cut square onto a piece of thin cardboard and trace the curved line. Draw another curved line and complete the banana-shaped strip, making it narrower at one end and wider at the other. The wider end should not be wider than 1 inch (2.5 cm). Add ¼ inch (0.6 cm) on both long sides of the template, for the seam edges.

4. Use the template to mark banana-shaped strips on different fabrics that contrast the colors of the square. Cut them out. Plant a banana-shaped strip of fabric into the curved line of each cut square. Replace one section of each cut square with a different color from the same stack.

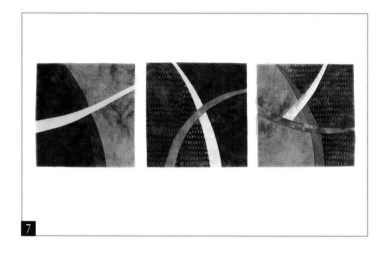

7

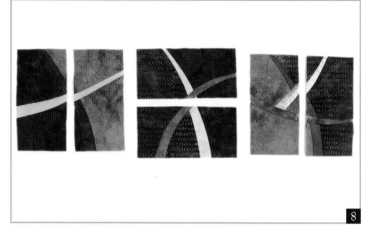

8

5. Machine piece the three parts together to make a tricolored block of fabric. Press the wrong side of each block, pressing the seam edges on either side of the banana-shaped strip onto the adjacent pieces of fabric.

6. Stack all tricolored blocks in groups of three. Cut them into two sections, again using a curved line. Orient this curved line in a different direction than the curved line cut in step 3. Repeat steps 4 to 6 with all blocks. Make new templates for the new banana-shaped strips.

7. Machine piece the parts and press on the wrong side of the four-colored blocks. Adding a third banana-shaped stripe to some of the blocks is possible at this stage. Straighten the edges of all blocks using a rotary cutter.

8. Cut the square blocks of fabric in half, to make rectangles. This allows for more diverse and interesting options when assembling the quilt top.

9. Arrange the rectangular units both horizontally and vertically in a diagonal graded-color composition, starting with the darkest through medium to the brightest.

10. Create an inner square of rectangular units with a color arrangement that contrasts the background surface, and adds a sense of depth and richness to the quilt.

11. Machine sew all rectangular fabric units together. Press the assembled quilt top. Add fusible batting and cotton backing to the quilt top. Machine-quilt the three layers together with complementary banana-shaped quilting, using transparent thread. Add a 1 inch (2.5 cm) binder all around, two sides in dark color fabric and the two sides in light color. ■

REFLECTIONS, GLASS WALLS, LA DEFENSE, PARIS, VAR. 4

Hand-dyed and over-dyed painted fabric,
cotton, polyester, rayon; dyed, over-dyed,
painted, fused, machine stitched;
43 x 57 inches (109 x 145 cm)

*This series explores the concept of
reflection and how to capture the essence
of images that are not physically there,
images made of light and movement,
images that are infinitely variable.
What does the eye see? What does the
camera see? What does the mind see?*

BARBARA J. SCHNEIDER
Woodstock, Illinois, USA

IT'S THE STONES
THAT SPEAK

Paper, twigs, dye, gesso,
mixed embroidery threads;
hand and machine quilted,
hand embroidered;
40 x 37 inches (102 x 94 cm)

CHERILYN MARTIN
Nümegen, The Netherlands

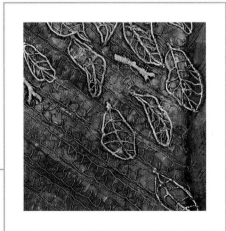

*Paper, just as seductive as fabric, offers
endless opportunities for surface design
and structural manipulation. I am
currently concentrating on the use of
paper as layering with mixed media
to build tactile surfaces with hidden
meanings. More recently, I have become
fascinated by the mysterious world of cave
temples and underground quarry systems.*

THE BUNGLE BUNGLES

Commercial and hand-painted cotton
fabric; fuse appliquéd, machine quilted;
50 x 36 inches (127 x 91 cm)

BETH MILLER
Kambah, Australia

*The striped domes of sandstone and
rough conglomerates of the Bungle
Bungles in the Purnululu National Park,
Western Australia, attract many visitors
every year. Although these formations
were well known to the local people, the
park was only "discovered" in 1987.
The Bungle Bungles were added to the
World Heritage List in 2003.*

GLEAM

Cotton; dye painted, discharged and soy-wax
resisted, machine pieced and quilted;
35 x 35 inches (89 x 89 cm)

JANET TWINN
Surrey, United Kingdom

*This work is part of a series inspired
by my local landscape. I enjoy
following the same path through the
woods, observing and documenting
changes in seasons. There is something
reassuring, despite ever-current
concerns about global warming, in
tracking the cycle of the year through
decay and regeneration.*

ART NOUVEAU KALEIDOSCOPE

Commercial and hand-dyed cottons;
fused, machine appliquéd, machine quilted;
40 x 40 inches (102 x 102 cm)

JEANNE IVALDI
Lake Maggiore, Italy

In a flea market in Switzerland, I came upon a stack of ladies' craft magazines from Paris dating from the early 1900s. I bought them all. At home, I lingered over the musty pages and was transported back in time. The art nouveau designs were transformed into motifs for this quilt. The magazines were in black and white, so I used rich colors to infuse the images with life.

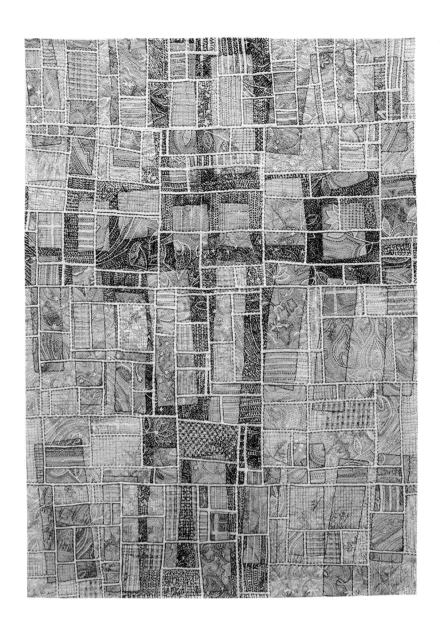

CROSSOVER

Commercial cotton and synthetic fabrics
with applied designs, polyester fabric
shapes, cotton embroidery threads; French
seamed patchwork, handstitched;
34 x 44 inches (86 x 112 cm)

MARY RUTH SMITH
Waco, Texas, USA

*This quilt is about transparency, fabric
overlays, intricate pieced construction
and detailed handstitching. The symbol
of the cross mimics and reinforces the
construction lines developed when the
small patches of fabrics were sewn
together. This method of piecing was
inspired by the intricately pieced wrapping
cloths made by Korean women during the
Chosun Dynasty (1392–1910).*

THINK OF THE MOTHERS II— THE VIOLENCE

Silk, synthetics, cotton, organza; hand dyed, hand painted, photo transferred, stamped, machine pieced, machine quilted, hand quilted, machine appliquéd, reverse appliquéd; 39 x 39 inches (99 x 99 cm)

There are so many different kinds of violence in society by which young people are killed. You can also see young women being trained as killers. This feels so unnatural: Women are supposed to bring forth life, not death. The quilts in this series are not a political but a social comment.

MIRJAM PET-JACOBS
Waalre, The Netherlands

MAKE THIS NIGHTMARE END

Hand-dyed and commercial cottons, cotton thread, cotton/poly batting; machine pieced and appliquéd, machine quilted; 32 x 62 inches (82 x 158 cm)

SHAWNA LAMPI-LEGAREE
Yellowknife, Northwest Territories, Canada

As part of the series called She's Coming Undone, *this quilt represents the period in the crisis where she wants to close her eyes to make it all disappear. She wants to deny that the crisis is happening to her. The eyes in the background are either watching her and making her feel vulnerable or looking away and giving her a sense of being invisible to those around her.*

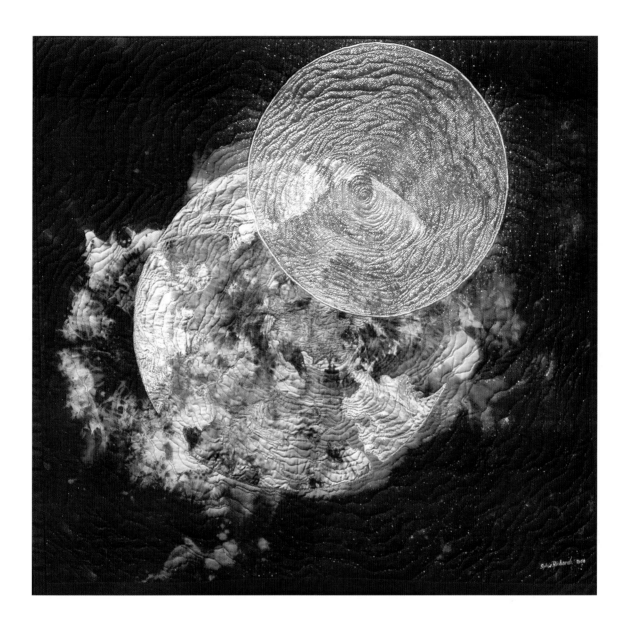

PARTIAL ECLIPSE

Indigo cotton, shot organza, wholecloth;
freely discharged, appliquéd,
freestyle machine quilted;
44 x 46 inches (112 x 117 cm)

SYLVIA RICHARDS
Stresa, Italy

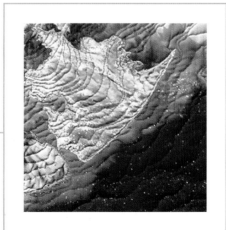

*A vision of planet earth, partially eclipsed
by the moon, inspired by photographs
taken by astronauts in space. This quilt
expresses the immensity of the universe,
with a dark background interrupted by
nebulous patches of gaseous materials.
The asymmetrically placed spheres, the
moon in shot organza partially eclipsing
planet earth, hover in space.*

ROOMS OF DISCOVERY

Hand-dyed homespun cotton;
hand dyed, machine pieced,
machine appliquéd, machine quilted;
50 x 36 inches (127 x 92 cm)

RUTH DE VOS
Mount Nasura, Western Australia, Australia

My children love nothing better than to visit the "dead animals" at the local museum. We take our sketchbooks and enjoy a journey of artistic and scientific discovery. What a wonderful world God has made! My artwork flows from my passion for God's creation and my ever-increasing awareness of the glory in the design, creation and preservation of the natural world.

AUTUMN ENCHANTMENT

Cotton, tulle, luminescent fibers, paint;
small pieces covered with tulle, machine
embroidered, machine quilted;
67 x 89 inches (170 x 226 cm)

NORIKO ENDO
Setagaya-ku, Tokyo, Japan

This quilt is part of a recent series of naturescapes. I love to walk into the woods. Birds and squirrels are my best friends. While walking in the woods, I enjoyed listening to the sound of falling leaves and the whispering of the birds.

STINKO QUILT

Cotton fabric, cotton batting, fabric paint,
cotton embroidery thread; wholecloth
painted, quilted, hand embroidered;
30 x 38 inches (76 x 96 cm)

PATTY HIEB
Seattle, Washington, USA

*As a volunteer at my local botanical
conservatory, I am inspired by the many
plants I work with. The biggest and
most famous is the* amorphophallus
titanum, *or corpse flower. Indigenous to
Sumatra, its blossom can reach a height
of 12 feet. Along with its enormous size,
it is known for a fragrance that travels
for miles and smells of rotting flesh.*

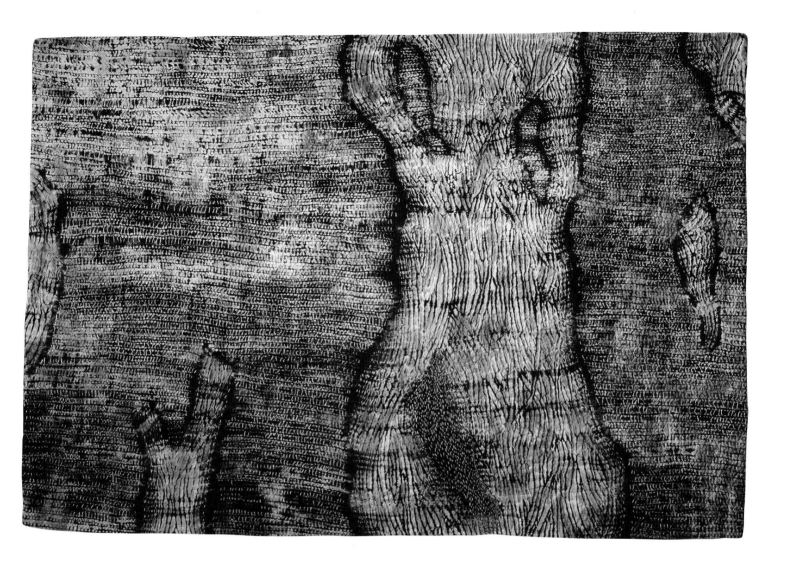

ORI-KUME #11

Cotton sateen, fiber reactive dye, silk
and cotton floss, synthetic micro-cord,
cotton backing and batting;
stitch-resist shibori patterned, dye
painted, layered, stitched;
46 x 31 inches (117 x 79 cm)

SUE CAVANAUGH
Columbus, Ohio, USA

*I am interested in life choices, in the
limitless paths we could choose each
day, the unexpected encounters, the
chances we take that enrich our lives.
Stitch resist shibori allows me to explore
these ideas. The final work has stitches
next to marks left by stitches that have
been removed, similar to laugh lines on
a face or a quirky line in the landscape
carved by a river.*

LAY OF
THE LAND II

Cottons, sheers, paint, thread,
digitally printed images;
hand stitched and appliquéd, raw-edge
machine appliquéd, fused, painted;
94 x 51 inches (239 x 130 cm)

VALERIE S. GOODWIN R.A.
Tallahassee, Florida, USA

In this quilt, I use a technique known as composite drawing as a way of interweaving graphic elements such as aerial views, plans, sections and elevations in a cohesive and creative way. The composite drawing relates back to the Beaux Art Analytique where several types of drawings related to an architectural project are carefully composed on one sheet.

NOTHING IS THE SAME, VI A AND B

Cotton, silk, paper; stitched dyed;
59 x 26 inches (150 x 66 cm)

ELS VAN BAARLE
Dreischor, The Netherlands

*Remains of structures ravaged by wind
and weather offer compelling observations.
Subtle colors and textures on the surface
of the cloth correlate to the layers of wax,
dyes, paper and threads. As an old wall
reveals a treasure of details when observed
up close, so does my cloth. What appears
at first glance to be one color becomes a
layer of nuances when studied in detail.*

FALLING APART, YET HOLDING TOGETHER JUST FINE!

Hand-dyed, bally batik and commercial
cotton fabric, cotton batting; machine
pieced, machine and hand quilted;
30 x 40 inches (76 x 102 cm)

*My work consists largely of art quilts,
but makes abundant use of traditional
structures as a point of departure that
I harness to the expression of my own
feelings and ideas. One of the things I
love about quilts is the softness of their
touch, so I try to piece rather than fuse
whenever I can.*

DANIT ROFEH
Tel Aviv, Israel

REGENERATION

Cotton, linen, silk; pieced, stitched,
constructed, mounted on hidden frame;
86 x 64 inches (218 x 163 cm)

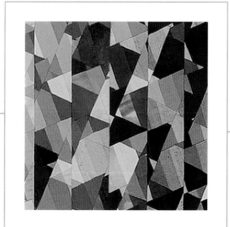

JOY SAVILLE
Princeton, New Jersey, USA

How does one express the very thin line between life and death, or the vastness of being that encompasses both life and death? It is the depth of these extremes that has informed my work since my husband's death in 2006.

ARTIST INDEX

JUDITH TOMLINSON TRAGER
Boulder, Colorado, USA
Page 27

CÉCILE TRENTINI
Zurich, Switzerland
Page 135

JANET TWINN
Surrey, United Kingdom
Page 144

ELS VAN BAARLE
Dreischor, The Netherlands
Pages 118, 155

DIRKJE VAN DER HORST-BEETSMA
Hoevelaken, The Netherlands
Pages 62, 87

GRIETJE VAN DER VEEN
Oberwil, Switzerland
Page 39

ELS VEREYCKEN
Hasselt, Belgium
Pages 52, 99

NELDA WARKENTIN
Anchorage, Alaska, USA
Page 56

LAURA WASILOWSKI
Elgin, Illinois, USA
Page 90

BARBARA W. WATLER
Hollywood, Florida, USA
Pages 36, 77

MAGGIE WEISS
Evanston, Illinois, USA
Page 114

NANCY WHITTINGTON
Chapel Hill, North Carolina, USA
Page 32

KENT WILLIAMS
Madison, Wisconsin, USA
Page 76

JEANNE WILLIAMSON
Natick, Massachusetts, USA
Pages 71, 101

AMIRA WISHINSKY
Tel Aviv, Israel
Pages 46–48

FIONA WRIGHT
Pushkar, Rajasthan, India
Page 96

CHARLOTTE YDE
Frederiksberg, Denmark
Pages 24, 51

ITA ZIV
Pardes Hana, Israel
Pages 28–30

PHOTO CREDITS